On bad ... ...oot-
ings on ... ...on
good nig... ...t's
back par... ...gun-
shots in ... distance.

Cops in New York who know the different
precincts—Harlem, the South Bronx, Washington Heights, Bed-Stuy, and Brownsville—think that the 75th is one of the
worst. That's why it's known as "The Killing Fields." Civilians have all seen the
reports on television. Kids shooting kids
in high school. Drive-by ambushes with
a hundred or more rounds fired. Innocent victims, sometimes infants, caught
in the crossfire over drug locations. East
New York is a war zone; a no-man's land;
a battlefield. It is *the ghetto*.

I have tried to tell the truth. I've tried to
tell the story exactly as I remember it, not
as I would *like* to remember it or how others would like me to tell it. What I hope
is that I've captured a measure of the reality of a place that should never have been
allowed to happen.

BROOKLYN BOUNCE

THE TRUE-LIFE ADVENTURES OF A GOOD COP IN A BAD PRECINCT

JOE POSS AND HENRY R. SCHLESINGER

AVON BOOKS ◆ NEW YORK

BROOKLYN BOUNCE is an original publication of Avon Books. This work has never before appeared in book form.

AVON BOOKS
A division of
The Hearst Corporation
1350 Avenue of the Americas
New York, New York 10019

Copyright © 1994 by M. Joseph Poss and Henry R. Schlesinger
Front cover art by J.K. Potter
Published by arrangement with the authors
Library of Congress Catalog Card Number: 94-94340
ISBN: 0-380-77337-6

First Avon Books Printing: November 1994

AVON TRADEMARK REG. U.S. PAT. OFF. AND IN OTHER COUNTRIES, MARCA REGISTRADA, HECHO EN U.S.A.

Printed in the U.S.A.

RA   10   9   8   7   6   5   4   3   2   1

To Lieutenant Patrick Skelly, a *boss* who was like a father. Who encouraged my curiosity and supported my eagerness to learn "the job" as he had learned it. And who, at the end of the day, said, with a pat on the back, "Good job *lad*, go home."

ACKNOWLEDGMENTS

I'd like to thank Henry, who put up with my perpetual nit-picking, just as I did his chain-smoking, java-guzzling, and theories of absolutism.

And to acknowledge past partners for their patience, guidance, and strength: To Steady Eddie, a good teacher and friend. To Lisa B., an outspoken but honest cop. To The Riz, a good friend during stressful times. And to Rose, for her insight, hindsight, and sometimes, no sight. Thank you all—the knowledge has been invaluable.

Thanks to the original squad 3: Sargeant Skelly, Stormin' Norman, Davey D., Tommy the cuz', Steady Eddie, Jimmy, Timmy, Mike, Benny, John, Gary, Frank, Jack, Johnny the fish, Wayne, Tommy V., Chris the motorhead, and Mikey. The nine squad chart couldn't have been tolerated without you.

I'd also like to acknowledge the last crew of dedicated patrol cops on the late-tour, especially Squad A-2: Mugsy, Joey the clammer, Shakey Jimmy, Chucky, Drew, Chris the sensitive guy, Eddie, The skater, The waiter, The Riz(again), E.D. Powers, Frankenberry, Mira Mira, George the rookie, and Tommy and Al the merry pranksters.

And to all of New York's Finest who put their lives on the line 24 hours a day to make yours a better one.

Things in tragedy ought to be rendered apparent without teaching.

—Aristotle

KOYAANISQATSI ko-yaa-nis-qatsi (from the Hopi language), N. 1. crazy life. 2. life in turmoil. 3. life out of balance. 4. life disintegrating. 5. a state of life that calls for another way of living.

It's said a firearm "never hits the ground twice" in Brooklyn. When a gun drops, it does the "Brooklyn Bounce." Whether it's a police officer's backup revolver lost during a foot-pursuit or a slain drug dealer's expensive 9 mm semi-automatic, someone will snatch it up before it hits the pavement. It will vanish from where it fell from a cop's ankle holster or a dead man's hand. Because a gun means respect. And respect means survival, especially in *East New York*.

PROLOGUE

I WORKED in the ghetto. For six and a half years I put on a uniform, a nightstick, and gun—nearly twenty pounds of equipment around my waist—and patrolled the streets. I was part of a mostly white precinct, policing a predominantly black and Hispanic community. I was one of the two accusing white faces staring out the window of a blue-and-white Chevy or Chrysler on the midnight tour. Everyone we saw was a felon, future-felon, or victim. I was one of *New York's Finest*.

The precinct I worked in was Brooklyn's 75th, known for its record-breaking homicide, felony, and drug arrests. We were one of the precincts that boosted the city's murder rate. Statistically, we were off the fucking scale.

The "7-5" is 5.6 square miles of pot-holed streets, standing foundations, crack houses, and housing projects. It is a community marked by yellow and red-fronted bodegas with tin awnings and flashing lights, their windows plastered with beer and malt liquor signs in English and Spanish; by take-out restaurants, where bullet-proof glass divides patrons from employees; and by entire blocks of burned out buildings.

At night, with all of the honest people sealed into their homes and the businesses gated, the landscape is one of urban wreckage—tossed off possessions and forgotten people. It is everything the city and the country

1

has abandoned and wants to forget. Worse than a failure, East New York is an embarrassment.

But most of all, East New York is a place haunted by a better, more prosperous past. You can see it in the architecture of the abandoned buildings inhabited by crack heads. It's apparent in the disrepair of post-WWII row houses, fenced in by chain-link trimmed with razor wire. And it's revealed in a history that dates back to before the Civil War, when there were hopes that this remote section of farm and pasture land would one day rival the growing metropolis of New York City. In East New York, what was will always be better than what is, and, most likely, what will be.

Within the confines of the 7-5 live something like 155,000 people. On a typical "late tour" (midnight-to-eight) shift, there are twenty cops on patrol, which averages out to around two cops per 8,000 people. On bad nights there are three or four shootings on the midnight tour alone. Even on good nights, just standing in the precinct's back parking lot, you could usually hear gunshots nearby.

Cops in New York who know the different precincts—Harlem, The South Bronx, Washington Heights, Bed-Stuy, and Brownsville—think that the 75th is one of the worst and the toughest. That's why it became known as *The Killing Fields*. Veteran cops just call it a shit-hole.

You could be talking to a neighbor, an ADA (assistant district attorney), or meet another cop off duty and tell them where you worked, then watch their faces harden. Cops and civilians alike know the precinct's reputation. Civilians have all read the stories in the newspapers and seen the reports on television. Kids shooting kids in high school. Drive-by ambushes with a hundred or more rounds fired. Innocent victims, sometimes infants, caught in the cross-fire over drug locations. The general feeling is that East New York is a war zone; a no-man's land; a battlefield. It is *the ghetto*.

The truth was, for a long time I liked to see those faces harden. East New York and the 7-5 are a different world, far removed from Manhattan, Queens, The Bronx, and Staten Island. Though in reality, it isn't. East New York is part of the same city, just a subway ride or a bridge away. Only a few miles from the quieter precincts of suburban homes and glamour of the high-rent neighborhoods with polished "pretty-boy" cops.

Maybe there was even some pride mixed in there, watching those expressions change. Because if you're working in the ghetto, it means that you're owed some measure of respect by other cops, because a cop's job in a war zone isn't the same as in Staten Island, Queens, or Manhattan.

What it comes down to is this: every day that you're still "on the job" isn't a victory, but a small fucking miracle. It means that you're smart enough, tough enough, or just lucky enough to make it through another tour. It means that you work the toughest job in the toughest city. And for a guy from Shaker Heights, Ohio, a midwestern suburb of green lawns and a country club lifestyle, that meant something real.

You'll find that same strange kind of pride in everyone that works or lives in the ghetto. Drug dealers, thieves, and even the kids. People on both sides of the law respect smart, lucky, and tough. A drug dealer in the ghetto has to be tougher, smarter, and luckier, than one on the Upper East Side. But drug dealer or cop, the ghetto gets to everyone, one way or another.

Even if you don't live in the ghetto, you carry a little bit of it away with you, piece by piece. You absorb it into your brain. It seeps in through the skin, right through to your marrow . . . to the core.

It was a slow, sickening dose of ghetto reality that washed away everything that had come before in my life. The manners, values, and ideals that I'd been carefully taught seemed frivolous. The daily routine of my job made them irrelevant.

It didn't happen suddenly, but slowly. Most of my friends' and family's petty problems and concerns grew small and insignificant. Their disasters—divorces, car payments, mortgages, layoffs, missed promotions and vacations—seemed like inconveniences compared to what I faced every fucking day. What could those people tell me? What could be as bad as lives spent so cheaply and grown so low and mean through drugs, poverty, or bad luck that survival was all that mattered?

What my friends and family saw was a change in attitude. That's what I took away from each tour, attitude—rough-edged, sarcastic, and grim. For my family the transformation must have seemed dramatic. They saw discernable degrees of change with each infrequent visit home—like time-lapse photography. What seemed a dramatic shift to them was in fact an imperceptible process that raised a wall. People wonder why cops only associate with other cops. For me, it's no longer a mystery.

But even with other cops I became something of an outcast: eyed with vague suspicion, marked by a college degree, and coming to the New York City Police Department from "out of town." The NYPD is a hometown job, and I was from Ohio, practically Kansas for Christ's sake. In the end, perhaps all their suspicions and petty paranoia were well-founded. I began to write a book. A fucking book!

When I first mentioned it to a couple of cops in my squad, the rumors began spreading. Then came the questions. "Poss is gonna dime us" (tattle). "You're not gonna use, like, real names and places, are you?" A subtle fear began creeping into their tone. I was about to expose truths and facts about life as a cop. Things cops like to keep to themselves, hidden from the public.

I had become a member of the media.

Cops fear two things from the media: That they will probably just tell a bunch of the usual lies. And, that they just might tell the truth. Everyone, even the media itself, is most at home within that gray area between fiction and truth—at the center—where egos and consciences can rest comfortably. They want to be told and to tell stories of good guys and bad guys. And they want to be told that there is a beginning, a middle, and an end. They would also like a nice moral to wrap things up neatly. To live in such a reality must be a comforting thing.

I have tried to tell the truth. I've tried to tell the story exactly as I remember it—not as I would like to remember it or as others would like me to tell it. I hope I've captured a measure of the reality of a place that never should have been allowed to happen.

IT CAUGHT me like some fatal mistake. As if I'd turned my back on the wrong person or hesitated at precisely the wrong time. It happened like one of those cop nightmares that wake you up in the middle of the night thankful to be in your own bed. And worse, I never saw it coming.

I never saw that piece of debris in the road.

That stupid fucking piece of water-soaked cardboard that brought the rear wheel of my motorcycle skidding out from under me, stealing control, so that the throttle, shift, brake, and my own body's weight were suddenly useless.

The rear wheel spun for an instant, then found traction at an angle that sent me to the ground, hard. I didn't even have time to lay the bike down, much less push away from it. One moment I was cruising along, and the next thing I knew, the bike was grinding along the pavement at thirty-five miles an hour, my helmet bouncing against the asphalt.

Done in by a piece of trash. In Staten Island no less.

What followed next was a dislocated shoulder, surgery, sick leave, and physical therapy. But most of all, a few months to sit back and think.

I discovered that I had reached a point where I didn't want to do it anymore. I no longer wanted to work in the ghetto. Not because I realized it was hopeless—I'd already figured that out a couple of years before. I'd known it, but kept going, propelled by the daily momentum of procedure, habit, and expertise.

It was as if I'd been asleep for years and was finally waking up. Now, after six and a half years, I didn't want to go back out on the street. I wasn't afraid of it— the street was the job. What I feared most was processing a couple hundred more "collars" (arrests), securing dozens more crime scenes, and perhaps exchanging "rounds" (gunfire) in a few more shoot-outs. I was tired of riding the edge—tired of the nightmare. Tired of the lies.

Strange how you can survive, and not survive at the same time.

The evening I was to report back for duty was one of those beautiful summer nights, maybe one of two dozen perfect days New York has out of an entire year. It took an act of will just to leave the house.

I was one of the few cops who commuted to work by subway. Most of the cops I knew lived out in the suburbs of Long Island and commuted by car. A lot of them lived at home with their parents. They lived there, saving their money, until they got married. Often, their mothers ironed their uniforms and cooked their meals. When they did get married, they bought a house or a condo in the adjacent town and their wives ironed their uniforms and cooked.

I made it a point to live in Brooklyn. But Cobble Hill, though only a subway ride away, is like a different world compared to East New York. Cobble Hill is where the dock workers and old Navy Yard workers settled into brownstones and mews apartments. Mostly Italian, there's a few "social clubs" in the area, which generally means family (Mob), and it's a safe neighborhood. It's tree-lined and as close to a bedroom community as Brooklyn gets. Over the last few years, Yuppies began moving in, refugees from Manhattan.

By the time I'd walked the dog, it was a little after 10:00 P.M. I had maybe fifteen minutes to make the 10:26 G train. If I caught that, then my connection for the A train would get me to work on time.

The subway ride was part of a ritual. I used the train as a way of easing into "the environment" and getting my attitude right for the night ahead. Every night you have to settle into the job. The guys who drive into work do it during the first half hour of the tour—getting coffee and taking their time going to "a job" (radio call). For me it was the subway.

Even at ten at night, the trains were always packed. Everyone in the car putting on their *don't-fuck-with-me* subway faces—no direct eye contact—or hiding behind the day's paper.

By the time the train pulled into Shepard station, my stop, I was the only white passenger. The walk from the subway to the 7-5 Station House is a two by two—two blocks over and two blocks up. I had to pass a couple of drug locations along the way. The first was a group of Jamaicans hanging out on the stoop and in the street. Seven or eight guys with dreadlocks, wearing collar-buttoned silk shirts and dress slacks. "Natty" uniforms that say strapped (packing a gun). They're always lounging on the steps and against the wall drinking beer, toking (smoking a joint), and talking in low voices.

These guys are known drive-by shooters, but nobody's ever been able to nail them. The cops on patrol know their cars, Hondas and Maximas—phat rides (customized)—with tinted windows, alloy wheels, and custom detailing. But there's never been a positive ID on the drivers. That night, like every other night, I passed by, and a couple of them said, "How you be doing, officer," in thick patois accents. Always a polite acknowledgement. They never dissed (disrespected) me, never cursed. It was just another night in the ghetto. They were at work, I was heading into work. It was all part of the ritual. But by the end of the night, we could end up shooting at each other. And they'd whack (kill) me in a heartbeat, cold and calculated, without remorse. There was always that chance.

The 7-5's Station House was built in the seventies and takes up an entire city block. It replaced the original 7-5, which looks like a stone castle and still stands on the corner of Miller and Liberty Avenues, finding new use as a Pentacostal church.

The new 7-5 is a three-story structure, devoid of personality or any style beyond the functional. A nearly windowless rectangle, divided and subdivided inside, the place was designed to be sealed quickly and securely. On those occasions when we've had either blackouts or angry crowds gather in front, the desk sergeants positioned cops armed with shotguns on the roof.

The lobby and desk area are done up in green institutional tile and hard marble-like floors. The drop acoustic ceiling hangs just low enough to make you feel a little claustrophobic. The fluorescents tend to sputter, and on any given day there's four or five of them out. And always, there's enough people talking at once to create a low roar. It looks and sounds like chaos.

After years in the precinct, I was able to break the confusion down into its discreet parts, discerning between the patterns of process and procedure. Patrolmen, anti-crime (plain clothes) cops, and maybe TNT (Tactical Narcotics Team) are all doing their thing. Everyone's looking after their own shit—their own prisoners, their own evidence, their own paperwork. A couple of prisoners were handcuffed to the wall-bar, and a couple more were "rear-cuffed" (hands behind their backs) in the holding cell to the rear of the roll-call deck. The arresting officers were running their perp's (perpetrators/criminals) pedigrees for "wants and warrants" with the help of the computer operator. Everyone was following procedure, even the prisoners. It's an organized chaos of procedure.

On this particular night, the four-to-midnight shift was hauling in perps. Guns, money, and "Jumbos," "Minis," and "missiles" (different ways of packaging crack) were layed out in front of the desk sergeant who was counting the evidence with an air of bored procedure.

Fifteen vials and a loaded .25 caliber Raven automatic won't raise an eyebrow, but it will get the arresting officer eight or more hours of O/T (overtime). It usually takes something big, like a hundred vials and a Desert Eagle .44 Mag Auto, to get a rise from the desk officer.

The "desk," where the sergeant sits, is the gateway into "the system" for guns, drugs, money, and perps. It's an ominous piece of furniture, nearly five feet high and extending twenty-five feet or more in length, opposite the roll-call deck. It's the focal point of the first floor. I've always gotten the feeling that the front desk of the 7-5 was probably St. Peter's first assignment.

Before roll call it was more of the same until the sergeant brought us to attention in two ranks of ten and began reading off of his clipboard. Two cops to a sector (patrol area) and the sergeant said who caught the fixed posts (stationary), the foot posts, and house (station house) assignments, and informed us about our meal (what time you take your hour break), and ring (your hourly call to the precinct). A ring was a holdover from the pre-radio days of call boxes, when officers were expected to call and check into the precinct at an assigned time. Now, you check in over the radio.

All of it's conveyed in familiar repetitive shorthand. "Poss, Smith. Sector George. 2356. 04:30 meal. Ten ring."

That information structures the night. It tells you what kind of night you're going to have. You know sector George, what kind of place it is. Maybe even know the car by its number and how it drives. You even know if you're going to be hungry when you sit down to eat.

But through the whole thing, you find yourself only half-listening, absorbing the information without thinking. You wait only for what you need to know: you wait for your name.

After the sergeant's given out the assignments, he walks slowly down the ranks, checking for working flashlights, locking holsters, and poking each one of us in the chest, checking for vests. It's all part of the ritual.

I stood there thinking about this, my first day back at the 7-5, and hoped he wouldn't check for riot helmets. Someone, another cop probably, had boosted mine while I was out sick. Cops are the worst fucking thieves. Riot helmets, mag-lights, nightsticks, and hats. You can't leave anything lying around. And you can't confront them with it, either. The best you can do is steal something back of equal value. That's the play (thinking).

Fucking ghetto cops.

ROLL CALL ends slowly, everyone bored and numb with the routine. They've already crossed that line in their minds from paramilitary professional to give-a-fuck ghetto cop. You can see it in their faces. By the time the sergeant says "left face," most of the men are turned halfway, the second step becoming a shuffle out of ranks. On the command, "fall out, take your posts," they've made their first steps toward the desk.

From roll call we'd get in line for our portables (radios), drifting over in a loose group. Behind the desk, the station house officer (SHO) has already pulled them from the wall charger and tossed them into a plastic milk crate.

The way it usually works is that one partner from a sector goes over, signs out two radios in the log, and picks up the car keys. Guys are drifting in from the four-to-midnight shift, throwing radios and keys down across the desk before heading down to their lockers.

On most nights, the midnight platoon commander, a lieutenant (LT or Lieu), comes over to the desk and barks, "She's holding jobs!" Which means the dispatcher has unanswered calls stacking up. Jobs start to stack up at the change of tours. One of the LT's jobs is to keep the radio out of backlog. If the dispatcher goes into radio alert—which means she's been holding jobs for up to twenty minutes—she'll call the desk to advise them of their status. After twenty minutes of jobs stacking up, and new jobs being added every thirty seconds, the precinct will go into backlog. If the LT can't clear them fast enough, he has to write up a UF 49 (incident report) explaining why to borough command.

But this is like a game. When the LT shouts it out, he's trying to make eye contact and "volunteer" someone for a shit job. If a rookie's around, that cop will pick it up, then fly out the door to the lot to impress the LT. But it's a meaningless show of enthusiasm; naive brownnosing that will burn itself out in a year or less.

Older guys, when the LT picks one out, will raise their radios to their mouths as they head out the door, but never key the mike. It's a game nobody really wins. The dispatcher will come over the radio looking for someone to cover a job, but will get no takers. When radio runs start piling up she'll radio the precinct's patrol sergeant. *Then* people start picking up jobs, responding out of respect for the sergeant; because sergeants shouldn't have to pick up jobs, let alone cover any.

You hand your partner his radio, and decide who's going to be the operator (driver), who's the recorder, and which of you is looking for a collar (arrest) and OT. What you hear going back and forth is, "You looking tonight?" Some guys are known for it. Rookies who want the experience, family men and guys newly engaged who need the money. But the thing is nobody's looking for a collar right out of the lot at the beginning of a tour. The perfect collar for a midnight-to-eight shift happens at 7:49 A.M. At 7:50 the meter switches to OT and even a shitty narcotics possession collar or an assault, or a third degree family offense, can be worth five or six hours at thirty-five bucks per hour.

In the old days, when the precinct was jammed with jobs, you could pick your collars off the radio. But lately, that's become more of a gamble. That shitty collar you passed up at 1:00 A.M. might be the only action you'll see all night.

* * *

The police radios, *the portables*, are your lifeline out on the street. Without one, nobody knows your location or condition. In an emergency, the radio can be used to bring backup, fire trucks, EMS, or clock a combative perp over the head. They can literally save your life.

A lot of the veteran cops still like the old radios, sticking to the bigger, boxier, and heavier four-channel Motorolas; just like they won't give up their old-fashioned coca-bola hardwood nightsticks for the new fiberglass PR-24 sidearm batons.

With the old model radios, channel 1 was the 7-5 precinct and our sister precinct, the 7-3 in Brownsville. Channel 2 was point-to-point. You could hear the dispatcher and communicate with another car. But the dispatcher couldn't hear you, and your transmission wasn't recorded. You'd tell someone, "go to 2," if you wanted to talk to each other without it being recorded. Channels 3 and 4 were citywide; all five boroughs could communicate on them, and you could hear everything that was going on in the city. This helped when detail groups, such as Brooklyn North Narcotics, was working in one precinct for a night. They'd go to a citywide channel because they were doing an operation separate from the precinct. Even if their operation moved to different parts of the city they could still use those channels and not interrupt whatever was going on in the specific precincts they happened to be in at the time.

The new radios are sleeker, slimmer, and have twelve channels. One through eight are reserved for all twenty-one Brooklyn precincts. The other four are citywide channels, one of which is reserved for point-to-point transmissions not recorded through the dispatcher because the range is minimal.

The RMPs (patrol cars) are basically shells. They have no shotgun mounted in front. No special equipment. Nothing that can be stolen. The RMPs aren't equipped with built-in police radios, just the standard

FMs—and half the time they don't work. New York's the only place in the nation you can see police cars with wire hangers stuck into a broken antenna to get a better FM signal. There are a few FATN (a national motor vehicle database) computer-equipped cars, but not many. Why waste them in a shit-hole like East New York? Waste them? Hell, risk them. Cops have gotten out of their RMPs on a call and come back only to find the electronic computer that operates the ignition system, and anything else stealable, ripped out of the car.

Again, with cars it's a matter of personal preference. Some guys like the old boxy 4.3 Chevies. Others prefer the new bubble cars, the Caprices. The point is, you want to get a car, *any car.* A lot of the cars are beat to shit, dented, dinged, and showing rust. I've seen guys wire-up bumpers and wedge milk crates behind their seats—anything just to get a usable car. Not getting a car means getting a foot post or a fixer post, and nobody wants that. Without a seat you could find yourself guarding an EDP (emotionally disturbed person) or an injured prisoner in Brookdale Hospital for the night . . . or sitting in the precinct's vouchered-auto lot, fenced in by razor-wire and chain-link, guarding stolen cars.

The 7-5 is comprised of eight sectors that more or less equally divide up the 5.6 square miles and 155,000 people—Adam-Boy; Charlie-David; Eddie; Frank; George; Henry-Ida; King-Mike; and John-Nora. The worst sectors are probably sector George, which surrounds the precinct house itself and Eddie—Frank, which sandwich Pennsylvania Avenue, they're a little more run down than the others. But in every sector, it's pretty much the same. The population in each is evenly divided. There are corner bodegas in every sector. The problems are more or less the same: drugs, guns, robberies, rapes, murders, and disputes of every variety.

The exception is the Highland Park area of the precinct—that's Adam-Boy's sector—which is made up of huge colonial and Victorian-styled homes, surrounded by cast-iron fences trimmed with razor-wire. This is where the prosperous local businessmen, assembly persons, and third and fourth generations of die-hard residents live.

You don't always have to stay in the sector you're assigned. You can drive anywhere within the precinct, but it's understood that you handle the jobs in your assigned sector. And if another call comes up and you're close to finishing a job, then you pick up the next one in your sector.

The problem with the 7-5 is that it's one of the city's largest precincts, as well as one of the most crime-ridden. If the goal of police work is to eliminate crime, then forget it. What we do, every night of the week, is *respond* to crime and "chase the radio"—answer one radio call after another. Ideally, on the late tour there are twenty uniformed officers—ten cars—to patrol an area a little smaller than a third the size of Manhattan.

Picture Manhattan, from Harlem down to the World Trade Center, patrolled by sixty cops in thirty cars, and you'll get an idea of why there isn't always a cop around when you need one.

If a unit in a sector makes an arrest or responds to a murder scene, then there are eighteen available. Two arrests, sixteen available. If there's not enough cars, you find yourself doubling-up on sectors.

On a perfect night, when the machine's running smoothly, in addition to eight working sector cars, there's two unmarked robbery cars, and a non-priority car—SP10—for past crimes such as stolen cars, past burglaries, and other non-priority stuff that you don't want to waste a sector car on. And maybe you'd even have one or two "conditions" cars, which are floaters that can pick up anything in any sector in the precinct when all the other cars are busy.

Walking into the precinct's back lot, you can spot the older guys from the new guys right away. The new guys, only on the job a couple of months or a couple of years, are hot to hit the streets and change the world. When I first arrived at the precinct in the spring of '88, there were approximately 249 cops stationed at the 7-5—most of them veterans. A lot of the cops were 30, 35 or older. Now there's nearly 400 cops there—many of them not even 25 yet. It's like a youth organization.

Some of them are true believers with some kind of fire for justice burning in their guts, and gung ho enough for a taste of the action. Adrenalin junkies.

All that's a distant memory for me now. The old-timers take their time, easing into it. Just a few years at the 7-5 is all you need to learn the truth—it was there before the shift and it'll be there after the shift. It was there before you started the job, and it'll be there when you retire. It'll always be there. Ten jobs at the beginning of a tour, 500 jobs a month, 5,000 jobs a year—there's no end to it.

When I was new on the job, the sergeant would dismiss roll call and I'd grab a radio, jump in a car, and pull out the back lot. I'd take on five jobs before I ever cleared the precinct's back gate. "What're you holding, central?" I'd ask the dispatcher eagerly.

There'd always be jobs. You could pick and choose at the change of tours, when the four-to-midnights were coming in and the late tours were going out. It's twenty, twenty-five minutes downtime and the fucking mutts (perps) on the street know it. They know when they don't see cops on the street, it's opportunity time. The time during a tour change is golden for them. And that's when they schedule a lot of their crimes. So by the time you hit the street, jobs are stacking up.

And if the dispatcher's holding twenty jobs and you're a rookie, you feel like you have to do her a favor. "Do the right thing." Get out there, pick up the jobs. Fight crime. Lock those fuckers up. Take on five jobs, fight for the cause. Meanwhile, the older guys are usually saying, "Fuck that, after I get my coffee. Then I'll take a job, *one job*, in my sector, and when I'm ready to take it. And not just a bag of shit, either."

That's the point I was heading toward in the end. The sad thing is, a guy considered to have "time" now can have only two years on the job, but he's experienced a lot of shit. Until he finally says, "Fuck it, who needs all this stress." You can see them, 25 years old and burning out. Only problem is, by the time you see it in yourself, it's too late. The only guys still eager after ten years are those who need to make the overtime. Just before Christmas or annual vacations, you'll see guys hustling to make arrests for the OT. Nobody continues to act like a rookie. You'd have to be an idiot without a life, or a robot. Definitely not a normal person. You just can't, you'd burn out too quick.

Pulling out of the lot I saw a couple of four-to-twelve cops in the MOS (member of service) parking lot. They're dressed in civilian clothes, drinking beer and making plans to meet for more drinks someplace else. A few are starting up their cars to go home. A couple waved and lifted a bottle in a beery benediction as we drove by.

Then, just like the night before and the one before that, I'm back on the street. I can see the entire precinct in my mind's eye. It doesn't matter if I'm the operator or recorder. When the dispatcher comes over the radio with a "10-10 (general code) shots fired" and a location, my mind flashes to the address. I see the cross streets, the bodega on the corner, and know it's a drug-prone location.

The sectors, the streets, the stores after awhile become imprinted in every cop's brain. It's like an aerial view. You see the whole maze of tenements, projects, and intersections. You know which streets run one way and where traffic lights or stop signs are located. You know them like your own hometown.

Shaker Heights, where I grew up, is a long way from East New York. A long way no matter how you look at it. A suburb of Cleveland, Shaker, as the natives call it, is an affluent community. The whole city, all six square miles of it, is about the same size as the 7-5. But Shaker Heights streets are lined with large Tudor houses, manicured lawns, and maple trees. It's "Leave It to Beaver" and "Father Knows Best" suburbia.

It's the kind of place where you know your neighbors. You know who just bought a new car and what kind of gas mileage they're getting; but most of all, you know you're safe there. And that safety isn't bought cheaply. The residents are vice presidents, CEOs, doctors, lawyers, and bank executives. Around 30,000 people live in Shaker, year to year the census doesn't change much; neither do the crime statistics. For one year in the early nineties, there were 1,434 felony offenses reported, including homicide, rape, robbery, aggravated assault, burglary, larceny/theft, motor vehicle theft, and arson. More than 1,300 of those were for burglary, motor vehicle theft, larceny, rape (one), and drug violations (sixteen). The police are diligent—they average more than 1,300 stops of suspicious persons and incidents a year.

By comparison, in 1993 East New York logged more than 129 murders. Years ago, someone in the Precinct's homicide detective squad put an old bakery counter above the door. "Now Serving 87, 88, 89," every time someone was killed, they'd advance the number.

That one year broke the record for the most murders in a single precinct in the history of New York City. For the same year, the entire city of Boston had around a hundred murders. That same year, the 7-5 had 3,181 robberies, 115 rapes, and 1,508 felony drug charges. These are more than statistics. For every violent crime and felony arrest, somebody's—and often entire families of somebodies—world was rocked or shattered, or left less than it was before.

With only a few exceptions, almost all the residents in Shaker Heights are white and upper middle class. You can live in Cleveland Heights or University Heights, which are just as nice, but it's understood that once you've moved to Shaker, you've arrived socially and financially.

My family lived comfortably. I grew up without fear, riding my bike in the street in the spring and waging snowball wars with other kids in the winter. My biggest fears were flunking math and being disciplined by teachers.

I remember the cops in Shaker vividly. Maybe all kids in the suburbs look at cops the same way. From the time you're a little kid in a place such as Shaker, you learn that a police officer is your friend. If there's smoke or fire, call the police. If you're in trouble, call the police. He's there to help and protect you. He's there to catch the bad guys. It's programmed into you.

But there's also a bit of novelty and fear surrounding cops in the suburbs. Almost every adult male you see wears a suit and tie and carries a briefcase, except cops. The car, the uniform, the gun, especially the gun—there's a fascination in it for little kids. They're like the cops on TV, people to be respected. Like a child looks up to his father.

One incident in particular, really stands out in my mind. I was 10 or 11 and had the opportunity to buy some firecrackers from another kid. Back then, it was an illegal transaction of the highest order, a kid's version of a major felony, maybe even made sweeter because it was illegal and dangerous. The other kid's parents had probably brought them back from down south, where they were legal. But in Ohio, they were prohibited.

It was late afternoon on a Saturday in the early summer. To this day I remember the temperature as cool, in the upper seventies. There was a slight breeze that carried the clean scent of fresh cut lawns. I was setting off firecrackers in the street with a couple of my friends. We were getting ready to put the match to another when someone spotted the police car. The matches, the fire-crackers, everything disappeared into our pockets as a genuine silent fear hit us. The cops!

I remember turning to the kid nearest me and whispering, "Don't squeal! Don't say anything!"

We all stood at the curb, watching as the cruiser pulled up. Now, I can imagine us looking just guilty as hell. Three kids standing around with their hands in their pockets, pale with fear.

The police in Shaker ride one man to a car. The offic-er sat in his royal blue car with the gold winged emblem on the door and crooked a finger for us to come to him. Walking over, our eyes focused and lingered on the shotgun mounted vertical to the dash. Then the ser-vice revolver, handcuffs, and mysterious black pouches on the wide belt. His uniform was neatly pressed, every crease in place, and his shoes were shined. Everything squared away.

Shit, this was serious, the real thing. The police had come after us with shotguns, pistols, and handcuffs, wearing a uniform and driving a nice clean car. The kind of car and cop that the Shaker taxpayers could afford.

All around, drapes were being pulled back, house-wives peeking through windows, some of them ven-turing out onto their porches. What could the police be doing on *their* street?

"We got a report someone was shooting off fire-crackers," the officer said. "You kids hear anything?"

I remember holding my breath, hoping none of my buddies would tattle on me in the face of such obvi-ous authority. Nobody said anything. The radio in the car crackled with static and calls. Finally I said, "No, we didn't hear anything, officer."

I could feel my buddies tensing, and why shouldn't they? I'd just lied to the police. I'd lied to one of the "Adam-12" guys, Reed or Malloy. Nobody ever lied to the police and got away with it. Serious penalties were no doubt in store. I had just made it worse on myself in the long run, as people always say.

"Okay then," the officer said, nodding stiffly. Then added, "I don't want to have to come back here."

I thought about it a lot that night. I was, unbelievably, troubled by conscious. I had gotten away with a lie. I'd crossed some line by lying to authority. And it felt shitty, but right after that cop left, we lit off some more firecrackers.

In comparison to my life as a cop now, that scene is almost laughable. In that stupid little incident was a small piece of the street, right there in Ward and June Cleaver's wood-trimmed, Ford Crown Victoria station wagon and Cadillac suburbia. He was probably a relaxed suburban patrolman, his routine interrupted by a nervous housewife, a taxpayer, calling. And he made a little show of it too, questioning us so the caller, from whatever window she was peeking out from, could see he was doing his job.

Today, if someone called 911 and reported kids shooting off firecrackers in the street, I can't fucking imagine what would happen. By the time a unit showed up, the kids would probably be old enough to vote.

See, this is the way it is for every kid who doesn't come from a cop family; you see the uniform, the gun, the car, the badge—all the symbols of respect and authority—and you think that by putting them on, they somehow transform you. Somehow they make you better than you are, stronger, smarter, braver . . . *something*. And that wouldn't be so bad, except every citizen you meet believes you to be either better or worse than anyone possibly could be. When you actually put all the symbols and tools of authority together, you find that behind them, it's still you.

TO BE a cop in New York City is to dwell in a different world. It's to see meanings of things, to live behind the headlines and the small news stories. Even more than a vantage point, it's to live in a culture of acronyms, profanity, and quick pronouncements. To be a cop is to laugh at odd times, finding grim humor in a stranger's tragedy. It's coming to expect that awkward silence when you tell someone you've just met off-duty that you're a cop. To be a cop in New York City is, to a large degree, to be an outcast. You do the job that nobody else wants. And you do it for not much money.

A lot of school janitors make more than cops. And, under a new contract agreement sanitation workers negotiated with the city, they now make more than cops. That sent a wake-up call to cops in New York; it confirmed what the people thought of them.

When you meet people and tell them you're a cop, they might say, "I could never do your job." What they mean is, "I wouldn't want your job, pal." But ninety-nine percent of the time, they're right when they say they couldn't do it.

Being a cop is also to walk around with a feeling of *superiority*, not because you wear a gun and a uniform, but because *you know*. You know all the city's dirty secrets. You see the patterns that appear random to everyone else.

You know the unbelievable degree to which people can be bad, ruthless, and stupid. You know how low and how quickly people can slide in society. But most of all, for better or for worse, you can feel just how tenuous our grip on society's constraints are. And when you work in the ghetto, you feel that grip loosening a little more each day.

You know it because you've seen it. You've seen the bodies on the sidewalk, in the street, and in the morgue. You know what fists, knives, bullets, and automobile accidents can do to living flesh. You know what drugs can do to once-functioning people. And you fucking well know the consequences of poverty, racism, and hopelessness. You've seen it, smelt it, processed it, and waded in it up to your badge. It is, in a very real way, the thing that occupies your mind. Even in quiet moments, it is the place to which your thoughts return.

As cliched as it sounds, you can't understand any of it unless you're a cop. You can be the wife, brother, sister, mother, or father of a cop, and still not understand. You can't know from just hearing second-hand stories.

You see the families of cops at social functions, and the spouses always hang back, just outside a tight little knot of cops. The wives, the children, the cousins, and in-laws, they're all in the background, never on center stage. It's the same way for female cops. Their husbands may be standing next to them in a small group of other cops, but they're not saying much, because even they don't know. And although the cops love their families, they still view them as outsiders. They are not a part of a cop's life in uniform. *Cops don't want them to be part of their lives in uniform.* They want to keep all the painful, dirty secrets to themselves. They want to protect their families' innocence. But it's a terrible fucking price they pay for it. And cops, on some level, still view their wives, husbands, and kids—all of them—as part of that huge misinformed mass of *civilians*. They just don't know, and they'll never understand.

I distinctly remember the first time I wanted to be a cop. I was a senior at Providence College working my way through a dual major in Sociology and Law Administration. Those were the majors you took when you were looking ahead to law school. That was the course I was on. It was the course that had been layed out for me from kindergarten: prep school, private college, and possibly law school. After that, I'd either be a pin-striped lawyer at a high-powered firm or a suit-and-tie executive at a major corporation.

As my senior year arrived, so did my senior thesis project. It's funny how even the smallest choices you make can change the whole direction of your life.

As part of my project, I decided to ride with ten separate police agencies throughout Rhode Island and write a paper on the experience. I didn't put a whole lot of thought into the topic. I wasn't naturally attracted to police work. Nobody in my family had ever been a cop. At the time, it seemed like a good alternative to spending hours in the library researching some dry topic such as the Supreme Court or the history of anti-trust laws. It also, to be perfectly honest, looked like an easy *A*.

Then along came Frank and "Shine," two cops from the Providence Police Department. Frank was an ex-marine, a big Italian guy, and Shine was a stocky black guy with a shaved head. They'd been partners for years and knew each other's every move. To this day, after six and a half years on the job myself, their team work still impresses me.

Maybe they just wanted to shock the kid from the local Catholic college, or maybe they saw something in me that I didn't see or recognize at the time. Maybe I reminded them of themselves at an earlier age. But these two cops took me under their wing and showed me what the job was about, really about.

One night around three in the morning, we were riding on patrol and a call came over the radio for a stolen car that another unit was pursuing. Frank was the operator, and Shine was the recorder. Anyway, the two vehicles whizzed by in a blur. First the stolen car, then the police car, lights flashing and sirens doplering. Frank punched the gas and we pulled out from the side street, joining the pursuit. Back then, I didn't know it, but Frank was one of the best wheel-men around. His driving was just incredibly precise. Like everything else he did, it exuded an extraordinary confidence. He knew exactly how the chase would end; it would end exactly the way he wanted it to.

We chased the car at a hundred miles an hour down one-way residential side streets, industrial service roads, and highways. The whole time, I was in the back with my knees against the front seat, nose right up against "the cage" and looking down the hood, watching the yellow line in the road disappear under our car. I could feel the speed in every bone of my body.

Shine was just sitting back, watching the scenery whip past, talking slow and relaxed. Occasionally he'd go over the radio to give our location to the dispatcher or offer some small piece of advice to Frank.

And there was Frank, driving at Indianapolis 500 speeds, with total self-assurance and concentration. No panic. No false moves. He was absolutely in control of the car. For both of them, it wasn't a question of "if we catch them." It was "when we catch them." The only unanswered question was how it would happen. I was like a kid in a candy shop. We were breaking the law. Breaking every traffic code in the book to catch someone who was breaking the law. For a college kid from the suburbs, this was the most real thing I'd ever experienced.

Finally, after about twenty minutes, the perps wiped out, totalling a parked car on a dead-end street. Instantly, the doors to the stolen car flew open and the two perps ran. Shine, being the recorder, was the hitter. He opened his door before we stopped and was out and running. Frank threw the car into park and was right behind him. The perps got about ten yards before Shine and Frank caught them and had them on the hood of the stolen car in cuffs.

I drove with them a few more times, partly for the senior project, but mostly because I enjoyed it. I'd caught the bug bad. I wanted to keep my adrenalin up, and I was willing to use any excuse I could to do it—even school.

These guys were administering the law. What they were doing was real. They were catching the bad guys, handcuffing them, and taking them to jail. As far as I could see, from the backseat of their cruiser, they were making a difference.

Even more importantly, they had rocked my world. Just those few "ride-alongs" gave me a hint, a vague glimmer, that there was something out there bigger— much bigger—than my fenced-off world of green lawns and country club society.

My mother, who was always big on charities and "causes," had talked me into being a Big Brother while I was at Providence. I was matched up with Junior Brown, a young black kid who was deaf since birth. It took me months to learn how to sign so we could communicate, but I finally did. And I liked the kid. He was sharp, intuitive, and determined. We had some great times together playing basketball, walking around campus, and just eating in the school cafeteria. It was a real experience for me. I was making a difference in someone's life. Even though I was only a teenager, a kid myself, I was doing something important. We stayed in touch for years, I still hear from him once in a while, through a card or letter. But the important thing is, I was doing something positive and got hooked on it.

With Frank and Shine it was the same way, I got hooked. Here was a chance to do something positive—

locking up bad guys—exciting, and most importantly, something that would take me beyond the little world I had always assumed was the universe.

I kept the desire to be a cop to myself for a long time. It was like some secret that would reveal me as an oddity to almost everyone I knew. For the rest of my senior year I suffered in silence, putting off taking the LSATs and applying to law school.

When spring came, a career counselor from the school fixed me up with an interview at an insurance company. I showed up on time, maybe even a little early. A receptionist took my name and led me into a waiting area.

I sat in my new suit, new shoes, and new tie listening to the phones ringing and watching people walking around. This is what it was all for, all those years of private prep school and college. All those tests and exams. All the pop-quizzes and papers. This is what I had been groomed for, right down to the clean fingernails, perpetually parted hair, and carefully knotted tie. This is what it had all been leading up to, including those four years of grade school Friday nights at Ms. Batzer's dancing classes.

I sat in the waiting room, my eyes going from the Japanese meditation garden, just outside one large window, to the view of the offices through an interior window at the other end of the room.

It was one of those companies with an office area the size of an airplane hangar partitioned into cubicles. The place was a maze of earth-tone dividers under rows of fluorescent lights. There were only a couple of actual offices in the corners. How long, I wondered, did it take until you got one of those offices? Five years? Ten years? Twenty years?

Outside it was spring, and I could see the green grass and trees. There was a meticulous, unreal quality about the way the garden was arranged and maintained. Not a leaf or a pebble was out of place. It didn't look as if anybody ever walked, much less meditated, there. What would they meditate on? Premium rates? Risk exposure? Maybe on how to get one of those corner offices. That window was like a painting that the people in the office had stopped noticing long ago.

Looking back toward the cubicles, I saw this guy— just some guy in shirt-sleeves—rise like a drowning man coming up for air near the center of the huge room. Then, while he was standing with the dividers at chest height, he extended his arms over his head, stretched, and yawned for what seemed like minutes. I remember thinking to myself, it's ten in the morning, the beginning of a work day, and this guy, in his mid-20s was fucking yawning. He was already tired and probably counting the hours 'til it was time to go home.

And I knew, right then, deep down in my heart of hearts, that I could never work in a place like that. The whole place looked like slow death. I didn't want this. I didn't want to be put into storage. I didn't want gardens nobody ever walked in. I didn't want idle daydreams of would she/could she secretaries. I didn't want to live a third of my life in this soft-walled maze under fluorescents. I wanted something real and free of restraints. I needed to control my *role* in my environment.

I wanted to be a cop.

IF YOU'RE a white person living in the suburbs or Manhattan, or anywhere that isn't a ghetto, then you've probably never seen a ghetto cop—never *experienced* a ghetto cop.

When most people think of the NYPD, they think about Manhattan and midtown cops. Those cops are slick pretty-boys. Their uniforms and manners are as clean and polished as their cars. Their hair is coiffed. They're in the public eye and they know it. And, more importantly, their commanding officers know it. They know that taxpayers, the media, and people of influence live, work, and play in Manhattan. Midtown is about corporate headquarters, high-priced stores, high-rent apartments, and exclusive restaurants.

Manhattan is not only the city's economic, cultural, and power center, it's also ground zero of political influence in the city. Midtown is about networks of people—hundreds of thousands of relationships, huge invisible webs of influence where you never know who knows who, or who is related. Or who can make a telephone call and get you transferred in a heartbeat. The unruly teenager; he may be the son or daughter of a prominent attorney. The victim of a mugging, the wife of a television executive. And the shoplifter, a diplomat. The ass you kiss in Midtown may save your own.

A midtown cop isn't going to get out of his car and toss (search) some guy in a Brooks Brothers suit or his model girlfriend for loitering outside Tiffany's. How would it sound, even politely? "Er, excuse me Chad, Buffy, would you mind terribly putting your hands against the wall?"

In midtown Manhattan, just the hint of rudeness could shit-can a career. A guy could drop a dime (make a civilian complaint) so quick it would make the cop's head spin. And "the job" would, as they say, entertain it. Even odds would have him catching a heavy one (punishment) from the sergeant and a shit fixer (foot) post for the next month.

Midnight cops in Manhattan see people with money barhopping at three in the morning. They're Manhattanites or bridge-and-tunnel nightlife commuters, in from Long Island, Queens, Jersey, and points beyond. They're spending money, helping the city's economy. If you approach them at all, it's for disorderly conduct. And then you either adjust their attitude verbally or ignore them. It's light duty.

If you listen to the Manhattan radio calls, you're likely to hear some cop screaming for help because he's getting yelled at and finger-poked in a street fight. Not only is he calling in a 10-85 (officer needs assistance) for a fucking scuffle, but the whole city hears it. If a cop did that in the ghetto, he would end up getting his locker thrown into the showers, or "covered" (keyed-out) the next time he tried to transmit a radio message.

Now here's the thing that really gets to me. The brass knows this. They know what the job is like in a "light house" or "C" precinct (one without an abundance of criminal activity); and they know the way we do the job in a "heavy house" or "A" precinct such as the 7-5. They not only know it, but they take advantage of the fact. They exploit it. You go to a parade or demonstration in Manhattan and they'll have all the Manhattan cops on the front lines looking sharp. But they'll keep us Brooklyn badasses sitting in vans around the corner, waiting in the wings just in case things turn ugly.

Cops adapt to their environment. The ghetto transforms them. Nobody can live there without it changing them, and you can't work there without it taking a toll on your thinking. The ghetto, even more than a place on a map, is a state of mind, an experience, an attitude. The poverty, the abandoned buildings, the burned-out cars and dead-end lives imprint themselves on you. It's not a Black thing, Hispanic thing, White thing, or cop thing. It's a human thing.

Ghetto cops wear the rough-edged camouflage of the ghetto. It's slipped into their manner and into their thinking. It's ugly and it's hard, and outside the ghetto it would be seen as a failing. But inside, within the boundaries of poverty and wreckage, it's been turned around, twisted a hundred and eighty degrees, so that all the flaws are virtues. They're a street code that, translated, means the cop is tough enough and smart enough to survive. It means that he possesses the secret street knowledge that there's no hope for this place.

It is, without exaggeration, as much a part of the ghetto cop's uniform as his collar brass, shield, or blue shirt. I learned it slowly, the same way I learned the landscape, streets, buildings, and alleys. The way I learned about the people, the criminals, and the commerce of street corners. Soon it became a familiar and necessary piece of me. The crack houses and drug locations became as familiar to me as the Tudor estates back home.

The point is, you put the Manhattan cop and the Brooklyn ghetto cop side by side and you would see the difference. Look at a Manhattan cop and you'll see that he's got a shiny new Chevy Caprice bubble car with a computer, a neatly pressed shirt and one of those new waist-length jackets, creased pants, shiny boots, and a short-cropped haircut. Your tax dollars at work. Value for the money. That's how you get respect in Manhattan—by looking professional.

In the ghetto, I get out of my boxy, banged-up Chevy in my old nylon duty jacket with the leather patch on the right forearm worn through from rubbing against my gun. The top button of my shirt is undone, with the clip-on tie clipped through the buttonhole of my left lapel. And maybe a small Band-Aid covering my earing. There's a swagger to how I get out of the car. Watch the Manhattan cops get out of their cars. They're stiff, like RoboCop, hat always on and looking just a little uncomfortable.

Now, who gets the respect in the ghetto? I do. My car has battle fatigue. I have battle fatigue. I'm as pissed-off and stressed out as everyone else who has to work or live there. I've heard every stupid lie and know I'm going to hear them again. I'm as much a part of the environment as the bricked-up tenements, the garbage-filled lots, and the corner bodegas. I have made myself belong there. I am part of it.

Put me in Manhattan looking like that and people would say, "My god, what a mess," like I was some homeless misplaced cop.

In the ghetto, this is the way it works. You pull up to a drug location at three in the morning and toss the dealer, steerer, banker, and look-out under the Right of Common Inquiry. Why? Because they've disrespected you by not "stepping off" (walking away) when you drove by. You know they're running a drug operation, and they know you know it. And the respect they should show is to curtail business for forty seconds at the sight of you.

And if they don't, then you stop the car, get out, and toss them. And it's, "Yo! Motherfucker, take your hands out of your fucking pockets and get on the wall. Don't even fucking look at me, look at the fucking wall." If you said that in Manhattan, people wouldn't even comply, they'd just stand there shocked, or say, "Do you have to swear at me, officer?" Then twenty other questions.

With the drug dealers, what you're trying to do is program them into "getting it." *When I pull up to this corner, you walk. You walk when you see me coming. Okay, you're a new guy, these are the rules: This is my fucking precinct, and you better well fucking show me respect. If you don't, then I'm going to toss you. If you still don't, if you make me get out of my nice warm police car, or my nice air-conditioned police car, depending on the season, and make me put you against the wall, then I'm going to tear this fucking corner apart. Get it? You fucking well better.*

And you have to keep coming back, again and again, until they get the message. But if you make the threat, you better follow through; because anyone who doesn't back up their talk doesn't last. They don't get respect, and maybe they don't deserve it. Even if you have to discon the guy—lock him up for three or four hours at the station house, handing him a disorderly conduct "C" summons in lieu of arrest—he still got locked up in front of his friends, who saw you live up to your threat.

This is the respect every cop in the ghetto wants, and it's absolutely the very best you can hope for. You can't fight the whole system. That's the other reality. You take one drug location out, another takes its place. Lock up one dealer, he'll be out in a day or two. And you can't move against the bigger guys, because the bigger agencies: FBI, ATF, DEA have already claimed them. They've planned the press conferences where they put the evidence—piles of bagged cocaine, triple-beam scales, Uzis, and stacks of money—on a table in front of a podium bearing a federal seal. All for the six o'clock news.

The average cop's job at the street level is a repetitive ritual. There's no progress in busting a street-level dealer, it's just filling time. It's putting on a show for the honest public and maybe making a bit of overtime in the process. Street theater and OT.

Now, I'm coming from the perspective of a late-tour cop. The feeling is, there's no public out in the ghetto to see you at three in the morning. The only people who are going to see you are perps, and who gives a fuck if they think you're professional. The only thing they have to know is that you'll kick the shit out of them if they disrespect you, just as surely as they'd whack (shoot) an underling or rival who disrespected them.

The reality is, if you're wandering around at three in the morning in the ghetto, you're probably up to no good. The decent people that live in the ghetto, and many do, are asleep. And if they're up, they're not leaving their houses because they're afraid.

Do you have a right to be walking around at three in the morning without having some cop jump all over you? Fuck yeah! But overriding the rights, even the laws, in every cop's mind is the reality. The reality is in his face every day. He sees it, he lives it. And anything he does, more than likely, isn't personal. He depends on his view of this little piece of the world for his survival. He knows that if he makes a mistake by turning his back on the wrong person, letting his guard down or just showing something that can be mistaken for weakness, he can get hurt or shot dead. And he wouldn't die a hero. Other cops, after hearing the circumstances, would shake their heads and know that he "died stupid."

There's no political spin, social theory, or direct order that can change his mind. He doesn't have to understand it. Maybe he doesn't want to understand it. As a matter of fact, he'd be happy, fucking thrilled, just to survive it.

Once you pull the RMP out on the street, you're on your own. Every decision you make, from which way to turn at the end of the block to whether to pull over a suspicious car, can come back in ways you never imagined.

Part of it is an independence, knowing that the decisions you make are your own. That's one of the reasons I got into police work. The other thing is cops are always looking for "markers." They're the things that tell you what kind of night it's going to be. Is it warm or humid? Then people will be out on the streets, just hanging around and drinking. And drinking means fights. It can mean drunk and disorderly or a dispute ending in gunfire.

Is it the weekend? Do people have money in their pockets from payday? That spells opportunity, a robber's lottery.

Then you look at the people. There are a thousand different ways to tell if a guy's a criminal. The most obvious is when a bunch of guys on a corner spread out as you pull up. Everyone starts to walk. The guy who walks away and keeps looking over his shoulder is "dirty." You watch how he walks. You look at the arms. You can tell. Since holsters are rare on the street, guns are loose, hidden in waistbands and pockets where they can be pulled (drawn) quickly. Guys who are strapped (carrying) or holding a jammy (gun) will walk short, shuffling along so the gun doesn't fall out or down their pants leg. If the gun's at his side, then you watch the arm swing. One arm will swing naturally, while the other stays plastered along his gun side, pressed against it, concealing the bulge.

If you stop to question him and he bolts, both hands on his waistband, he's dirty. Some guys on the street will lift their shirts and turn 360 degrees in a slow pirouette, just to show you they're not packing. They know the routine.

Personally, I love gun runs, calls for an armed person. A gun is loaded. A gun is physical, undeniable, irrefutable evidence. Drugs and money, on the other hand, are a touchy situation. You can run after a person, and they can throw a gun away. But when you catch him, after scooping up the gun, you still have a case. But drug possession can be denied. And more often than not, perps dispose of drugs during a chase. Guns usually aren't disposed of. Drugs are product, but a gun means survival. A couple of vials of crack can be replaced, but a gun is harder and more expensive to acquire.

The drug trade involves money—and that makes cops vulnerable. It's a shakey and sensitive topic with the NYPD. Dealers regularly lie. If a cop recovers a thousand dollars, the dealer will claim it was two thousand, and the department will investigate his claim. He's a fucking criminal, but the department listens to him. And the dealers know they've caused the cop who busted them a hassle.

It's better to just pull up, take the drugs, toss them down the sewer, and cut the guy loose. Safer still, call a sergeant to the scene to verify the count (number of vials recovered), take the drugs back to the precinct to be vouchered, analyzed, and eventually destroyed.

Either way, the street-level dealer you just cut loose still has to pay for the drugs. The supplier gives them to him on consignment, so he's got to go back to his supplier and say the cops took the drugs.

The supplier is going to come down hard on him: "What do you mean the cops took the drugs and didn't bust you? Where's my money? Where's my drugs?" If that's the excuse the dealer has, time after time, he's in deep shit with the supplier. All the supplier cares about is his money, profit, and drugs. All the supplier knows— all he wants to know—is that he gave the street dealer $500 worth of crack and that $500 fucking well better come back in cash.

The supplier's only insurance against corrupt underlings is fear. He guards that fear jealously, maintaining it with any means at his disposal. Just to prevent a rumor that he's been chumped is reason enough to whack a street dealer.

Every supplier has a nine-millimeter Sword of Damocles hanging over his head. Because even a rumor on the street that a dealer can be chumped fosters speculation by competitors and their ambitious underlings that he's weak and soft. Maybe even too weak to hold his network of corners. That can lead to territorial disputes and corner shoot-outs. A good corner franchise is worth a grand a day or more in the supplier's pocket. And the only thing that keeps him there— free from attack and open for business—is fear.

Cops know this. We use it to our advantage. It's an attitude of: hey, if I can't eliminate the problem myself, why not manipulate the situation at least in my favor? Let them kill each other off . . . let them eliminate each other. If, for no other reason, territorial shoot-outs quiet a corner for a few days.

You can't rationalize it. It's a self-perpetuating game of false hope, dubious motives, and the basest form of justice. It's twisted. But true.

EVERY COP knows where drugs are sold. They know the faces of the dealers, the lookouts, the steerers. But it's tough to bust them. They have a system that keeps the stash and the dealers separate, guaranteeing that if anyone is busted, it's for possession and not distribution. What appears chaotic on the surface is a structured organization run with ruthless efficiency. It's a machine built on teamwork, designed to keep the drugs flowing to the street while minimizing the risk from cops and competitors. Fortune 500 companies should be run so well.

The first guy, the seller, takes the money from the buyer and ducks out of sight into an alley, unlit lobby, or tenement hallway. Once off the street, in a secured area, the seller passes the cash to the holder, who in turn gives the seller the product. The seller then returns to the buyer with the drugs. This division of responsibility insures that at no time is the seller on the street in possession of the drugs and the money simultaneously. From a legal standpoint, it's the difference between "possession with intent" to distribute and simply "possession."

They'll keep a quantity (say, twenty-five vials) out on the street, hiding them under a rock; in the trash in an old potato chip bag; or in a bodega's security gate track. When those are sold, they go back into an apartment building to drop off the money and pick up more crack. They'll do this during a shift change, when there aren't any cops around. But if business is particularly brisk and they have to re-stock, they'll call in a bogus "10-13" (officer needs assistance), giving an address at the other end of the precinct, assuring that every cop in the precinct will fly to that location.

For cops, a dealer's mere presence is an insult. Here are these scumbags doing business out in the open, and they're untouchable. And they know it. What's more, the anonymous, false "13s," they call in create a seriously dangerous condition for cops.

A couple of years ago, a bunch of us decided to do something about one location on Williams and Newport avenues, in an area called "West of Penn," west of Pennsylvania Avenue, the dividing line that runs through sectors Eddie and Frank. Dealers were selling drugs in front of a corner bodega, but the supply was coming out of a six-story tenement next door.

The problem with this building was there were empty lots to the south, the southeast, and the northeast. There just wasn't any way to sneak up on it. As soon as a cop showed his face, one of the lookouts would shout, "bahando," which is Spanish for "look out" or signal that cops are on the block with a two-note, high/low whistle.

The corner bodega was a small store with a large cinder block wall covered by graffitied murals. The detailed murals were testaments to guys who died on that corner. There'd be a painted headstone with the guy's name that said, "In Memory of" and when he was born and when he died. And along with his name would be something that he loved. I call them ghetto prizes. If the guy liked motorcycles, they'd paint a motorcycle alongside his name. If he had a particularly nice gun, there'd be a spraypainted gun. Or if he was a lady's man, there'd be a couple of women in the picture near his name.

The building had a double doorway of black metal, with small plexiglass windows covered by wire mesh.

Maybe five or six bullet holes in the door were left over from the last drive-by. The second door inside, leading from the lobby to the hall, was completely off its hinges. The hall was dark, graffiti covering the marble and plaster.

The guy running the operation was known as "Fat Man" or "Fats," something like that, because he was extremely large. He lived in the first apartment on the ground floor.

The place was untouchable. These guys were smart and organized. We stormed that corner half a dozen times and never came up with anything. But every cop in the precinct was sick of that fucking corner, and sick of the scumbags dealing there. Not only were these guys starting to disrespect us, by not walking away when we drove by, they were calling in "13s" left and right, and we all knew it.

When I worked four-to-midnights, a bunch of us got together before a shift and decided what to do about this location. We were determined to turn the tables on these guys. There were a lot of guns there as well as drugs. The idea was to hit them hard and shut them down for a little while. A perp definitely had to go. We were out to take guns and drugs off the street, and to put a body or two into the system.

This particular day we hit the corner three times. Four or five cars, a couple of footmen just being loud and dramatic as hell. We'd come racing up to the building and run into the hall. All these assholes saw were a bunch of cops, they never bothered to count bodies. After the third time, when everyone ran in, we had a few cops stay in the building and hide on the roof. One cop was on our division radio channel, the other was on point-to-point, which central couldn't hear.

A half hour later, we had a car roll by and toss the corner, putting everyone up on the wall to search them and pretend to look for drugs.

Somewhere on the other side of the precinct, a cop

phoned in a "13." The whole squad knew about it, and only a couple of cars responded. The main thing was, the dealers heard the call come over the radio. Instantly, the cops tossing the corner stopped, ran back to their cars, and screeched off.

It was maybe twenty seconds before the cops on the roof reported that the guys had recovered their guns and drugs from the trash and were going to re-stock their supply.

The RMP that had driven off to the bogus "13" did a sharp U-turn around the corner, waited thirty seconds for the cops on the roof to get back downstairs, and doubled back along with three other cars.

Everybody scattered as we flew out of the cars. One of the spotters saw the cars coming and went for his waist. But it was too late; four cops jumped him and started beating the living shit out of the guy, recovering from his waistband, a fully loaded automatic.

I was driving one of the cars, and as I came around the corner, I jammed down on the brake, opened the door, and pushed the gear shift into park—all in one motion. I remember having my gun out, drawing it as I brought my hand down from the gearshift and stepped out the door.

As soon as I was clear of the car, I saw this guy run into the lobby. I followed him through the door, gun raised straight up, down the darkened hallway, and toward the back door. He saw me and went for his waistband. Suddenly I'm joined by three other cops and we tackled him. For a split second after we connected, we stayed frozen like that, nobody moving. Then our weight and forward momentum pushed him tumbling back out into the building's walled-in courtyard.

As we hit the ground, four sets of hands kept his hand away from his waistband as he writhed and twisted across the concrete.

Two cops were trying to take the gun away from the guy, while another cop and I tried to cuff him. But he still struggled and wouldn't let go of the gun. This guy was strong. The other cop trying to cuff him finally stepped on his hand and got him to release the gun. It was a .380 automatic with a full clip and one round in the chamber.

By the time we got him to his feet and hauled him outside, I could see other RMPs filled with suspects.

Someone got on the radio and called a sergeant to the scene. We ended up with three arrests, two loaded guns, but no buyers or dealers. For all our trouble, the thing never went to trial. The defendants pleaded out. Fat Man got away.

But we'd done a bust without the brass knowing, so there was some sense of victory in that. If we had involved a sergeant, he would have wanted to plan the whole thing or at least be involved in it. The guy with the gun wouldn't have been jacked (hit) as hard as he was, either. And if the sergeant had heard what we were doing, everyone involved would have caught a foot post for God knows how long.

More than likely, if we had told the sergeant, he would have shot down the idea. Because if there was the smallest chance it could go wrong, cause him head-aches, or make more work for him, he would have backed out.

The corner quieted down for a couple of weeks, but then they just started up with the same bullshit. So we decided to hit it again.

Six or eight of us got together before roll call one night and worked out a plan. This time we decided to hit them in the dark. Two of the cars waited around the corner. I got out of the RMP, took my jacket off, and reversed it so they couldn't see my badge or gunbelt. Then I started walking up the street—just another white boy venturing into the ghetto to buy his drugs.

When I got twenty yards away, the spotter made me and went for his waistband. I pulled my gun and yelled, "Police! Don't move motherfucker!"

But the guy bolted into the building. As I ran into the lobby after him, I called it in. I could hear him running down the hallway to the stairs at the back of the first floor, and out into a back alley. I ran after him into the pitch black alley with my gun out as another cop came around the corner.

The guy had his gun out, saw the other cop, and reversed, jumping up and catching hold of a fire escape ladder to the abandoned building next door. Both of us were yelling for him to stop, but he kept climbing the ladder, the gun still in his hand.

I looked up and saw all the windows of the building were cinder blocked over except for a few. The guy then vanished into one of the opened windows.

Without even thinking about it, I started up the ladder. When I got to the open window the perp had climbed through, I peeked around the jagged edge, hoping not to get my head blown off. Inside, I heard him running up the stairs.

The other cop was right behind me by now, so we climbed in through the window. Inside it was dark; the only light seeping in came from the alleyway floodlight. It smelled like piss and decay.

"You got a flashlight?" I asked, because mine was still in the car.

"No," he said. "It's in the car."

I got through the window and ran across the room.

As my partner followed me through the window, I heard a sharp snap of wood, followed by him shouting, "Oh fuck!" The floor had given out under him, and his leg was buried to the knee in a jagged hole.

"What do we do now?" I asked.

The cop pulled his leg out of the floor and said, "Room to room."

"Room to fucking room!" I whispered back. "We don't have a flashlight. That asshole could have a gun on us now and we wouldn't know it. He can probably hear our radios."

I had one of those mini-mag flashlights in my pocket and pulled it out. By now my heart was going a million beats a minute. And I know, this is just fucking insane. But it was great too. It was the risk and adrenalin that kept us going.

So we started a room-to-room search, working our way up floor by floor in the darkness. And when we got to the top floor, we heard him.

I stopped in the doorway and yelled into the room. I couldn't see a fucking thing, but I could hear him rustling around in there.

The other cop, standing on the right side of the door, yelled in as I shined the mini-mag into the room. The beam was just strong enough to light up one corner. There was nothing in the room, just a closet where he must have been hiding.

I walked slowly to the other side of the living room, watching the closet. I and the other cop had our guns out. And were both yelling.

"Let me see your fucking hands!"

"If I see a fucking gun, I'm gonna blow your fucking head off!"

"Show me your fucking hands, motherfucker!"

With each step closer to the closet, I could feel my finger pulling back on the trigger, tensing, palm hard against the backstrap. And I kept hearing this rustling in the closet. What the fuck was he doing in there?

Suddenly, from downstairs, I heard, "Hey, where are you guys?"

"Up here! Top floor!" my partner shouted back, then added, "Bring flashlights!"

Twenty seconds later, we had four more guys in the room, lighting it up with flashlights.

All six of us started moving again on the closet, inching our way closer and closer. One of the guys stood back, off to the side and slowly opened the door, while the rest of us punched our guns and flashlights around the door jam.

From inside the closet, the guy yelled, "Don't shoot! Please, don't shoot!" An instant later, he stuck his hands through the door.

I pulled on one hand, another guy pulled the other, and together we yanked him out of the closet and threw him on the floor.

"Where's the gun? Where's the fucking gun!"

"I don't have no gun," he said.

"Where's the fucking gun, motherfucker!"

Somebody cuffed him and pushed him back down on the floor.

Using one of the other cop's flashlights, I looked in the closet. No gun.

"You find it?" someone asked me.

"No, I can't see it," I shouted back.

"I told you, there ain't no gun," the suspect said, and tried to rise up a little on his chest, turning his head over his shoulder to see the cop.

"Shut the fuck up," a cop said, then wacked the guy back to the ground.

By now, I was on my hands and knees looking in every fucking corner of the closet. No gun.

Then I saw this hole at the far end of the closet, in the back corner. It looked like a rat hole. I broke off a few more chunks of plaster around the edges and shined the light down into it. And there, just out of arm's reach, was the butt of a gun, wedged between floors.

"You got the gun?"

"No, but I can see it." I said.

"What?"

"It's in the wall."

"What the fuck are you talking about?"

Another cop came into the closet, and I showed him. Now we have a gun, but can't recover it.

Suddenly the sergeant got on the radio, "I want you out of that building, now!" There was no way in hell he was coming into the building. The front door was cinder blocked, and the fire escape was the only way in.

And he sure wasn't going to climb up that fire escape. Plus, he wanted to know just how we intended to get the perp out, him being handcuffed and all.

I'm only worried about recovering the gun. Finally, somebody showed up with a wire hanger. I untwisted it and worked the hooked end toward the trigger guard. As I pulled the gun out of the hole, I saw it was cocked.

It's another .380. Uncocking the gun and pulling the slide back, I cleared the round in the chamber. The guy could have shot us at any time.

By now, the sergeant was fucking livid, screaming over the radio as we brought the guy down the stairs. When we reached the opened window, we eased him back out onto the fire escape. Me and another cop held him by the collar and began lowering him down the ladder's rungs, one by one, with his hands still cuffed behind his back.

With two steps left, and a six-foot drop to the ground, we couldn't hang on to him—our arms were already extended as far as they'd go.

"Come on, let'em go, we'll catch him," one of the cops below said.

"Let go, we got him! We got him!" another cop on the ground said, actually reaching up.

We let him go, and the cops on the ground immediately stepped away as the guy fell into a pile of trash.

The guy was pissed off, but wasn't hurt. As we hauled him up and brought him out of the alley, I saw the street was filled with department vehicles—ten or fifteen RMPs: NYPD, Transit, Housing, foot cops, ESU (Emergency Services Unit), and EMS buses (ambulances). And they all had their turret lights going. It was as if we were hauling in all ten of America's Most Wanted, not just some gun-toting spotter from a corner drug operation.

My partner sat down on the rear steps of an EMS bus and pulled his pants leg up. It was soaked from the knee down with blood, and there was a huge gash in his leg.

And the funny thing was, after all that bullshit, he was afraid he'd have to get a tetanus shot.

In the end, we couldn't tie the perp to the drugs, but we got him on gun possession and he pleaded the case out.

Working steady midnights in the 7-5 is to witness "ghetto Darwinism" up close. It's a lesson in survival in a place where the big, the fast, and the smart eat the small, the slow, and the stupid.

As cliched as it sounds, a good cop knows the streets and the people in them.

You get so that you know which neighborhood bodega will front a crackhead twenty bucks for the family's VCR or pay cash-on-delivery for a "semi-warm" car stereo ripped out of a Saab in Brooklyn Heights or Park Slope.

On the street, you learn how a car is stripped. First the battery, then the tires, then the alternator, then the interior, and finally the engine.

Some of the things I've seen still bewilder me. Like just how strong a crackhead, at a certain point in their addiction, can be. They subsist on candy bars and other junk food, certainly not a well-balanced diet. Food and nearly every other basic necessity has been knocked off their top ten list of priorities, replaced by their habit. Yet these guys have virtually no body fat—they're all muscle—washboard stomachs, and toned arms. Six months later they could be skeletons—what cops call the "Jenny Crack Diet Plan"—but for a few weeks or months, they're dangerous.

Another thing that surprises me is how fast a fucking thief can run. They can go from a dead stop, crouching beside a car trying to break in, to Road Runner "beep-beep speed" in three strides. And they can maintain that speed for two, three, or four blocks, just far enough ahead of a cop to duck into the nearest alley or doorway. Then they just seem to vaporize.

I've learned how guns are best hidden in the bulk of "Triple Fat" goose down jackets ... or in the air bag compartments, under the fire walls, in hinged door panels, and armrest consoles of cars. I learned how the "Mister Softee" ice cream man, a familiar sight from my own childhood, could be selling drugs from his truck. And the more I learned, the more there was to learn. It seemed endless. The information required, just to survive, could fill an encyclopedia.

After a couple of months, I began to recognize the skells (homeless drifters) who push stolen post office bins and shopping carts through the streets. They look for bottles, cans, pieces of wire or aluminum—anything that can be collected and sold. These guys are out all night, burning tires, stripping the insulation from copper wire, filling their carts with scrap that they redeem for thirty-five cents a pound. Nobody ever pays them any attention, but in their nocturnal scavenging, they see things. They witness crimes. They hear the rumors.

One of the first things I learned when I was just starting out was that hookers, junkies, and skells are good sources of information. They have no loyalty to anyone.

The public is always surprised and gratified whenever a high-profile crime hits the headlines, and two or three days later there's a photo in the paper of detectives hauling the perps in. *Heroes*.

Cops and detectives in the precinct pursuing an ongoing investigation start leaning on people, street people, known dealers, hookers, skells—anyone. Somebody always knows something, or knows someone who knows something.

If it's a slow night, when you need the OT, there's always somebody doing *something* illegal. It's just a matter of ferreting out the information.

My first partner, Eddie, showed me how it worked. There was this one part of the subway-line that ran along Van Sindren Avenue. Before it was barricaded and gated by the city, junkies used to hang out under it and shoot up.

What we would do was wait in the RMP a couple of blocks away, watching in the shadows until they had the dope in the needle, then we'd pull down the narrow alley fast. They'd either panic and run or just rest the needle down and pretend to be taking a piss.

We'd jump out of the car, put them against the wall, and start asking them questions about who's dealing? Who's carrying (packing a gun)? And what, if anything, they've witnessed?

Usually, we got no answers, just a bunch of stuttering and stammering.

"You got a spike (needle)?" Eddie would ask, reaching into the junkie's pockets.

"No, no spike, man," always came the reply.

If we found one, then the lie earned them a crueller (head blow), because if you got pricked by the needle, you're fucked. Then you must take an AIDS test. But usually these guys told the truth, their spikes and works (paraphernalia used to prepare heroin) were set up, ready to be injected or resting nearby.

Any lack of cooperation resulted in our squirting out the hypodermic's contents into the dirt. We'd do it so they could watch. Twenty bucks on the ground. Wasted. His high and stability for the day soaking into the gravel. If we found a crack pipe, we'd smash it.

"Okay, every time we come back here, we're going to harass the shit out of you. Understand? We're not going to lock you up, we're just going to make your life miserable. Unless you give us information. Understand?"

Obviously, we were supposed to be locking these guys up, but if we hauled in one deck of heroin or two vials of crack, we'd be laughed out of the precinct. However, after a few questionings, the junkies would come up with information—legit information.

DRUGS ARE the major industry in the ghetto. The proceeds from street sales pay rents, buy groceries, and keep the lights and telephones from being shut off. What looks random and haphazard to the outsider is a mercilessly efficient business that keeps the supply cheap and available.

Surprisingly, the kids from the suburbs know it. A large vial of crack, called a Jumbo, might cost twenty bucks on Long Island. For a few bucks worth of gas you can buy the same vial for five bucks in East New York. It's the difference between buying two and a half versus five vials for half the price. It's the difference between buying wholesale and retail.

On a slow night, you can find a couple of RMPs parked in the shadows just off Crescent Street and Pitkin avenues, waiting for these kids from the suburbs. It's a well-known drug location, and a favorite with the white kids from Long Island. It's just off the Conduit Boulevard, which is just off the Belt Parkway, which connects with the Southern State to the Long Island Expressway. Express service. Easy in; easy out.

These kids want to spend as little time as possible in the ghetto. And at this particular location, they can do their business and be on their way back to Long Island in ten minutes or less. It's like a drive-up window at McDonald's.

51

There's a couple of ways to discourage these kids. First, you can pull up on the car and prevent the transaction. Jump on them as soon as they pull up. Go over to the car and start barking questions in their faces: "What the fuck are you doing here?" "Give me your license!" "What the fuck are you bringing your girlfriend here for?" "You're from Smithtown: Get your white fucking ass back to Smithtown; I don't want to see you here again!"

That's basically a scare tactic. It's good if it's a busy night and you don't have the time to waste on bullshit. The second tactic is to wait until he gets out of the car and walks around the corner to do the deal. Then give the girlfriend a toss—put her against the car and search her.

"Who's the driver?" "Who are you? Where are you from? Why are you here?" You give her the same routine as before, but now her boyfriend's probably done doing his deal and is hanging back in the shadows somewhere. He has no intention of coming near that car, not with the cops there, and especially not with a pocket full of crack or pot.

And you keep on her. Keep asking questions. You know he's getting sweaty, watching from wherever he is, because he's in the fucking ghetto. After a little while, you tell her to take the car and get the fuck out of there.

"If I see this car again, I'm gonna lock you up," we tell her. "We're gonna take the fucking car away and give it to the city as forfeiture, because you're in a known drug location."

She's scared. She's spent her whole life on Long Island and probably doesn't have a clue as to what cops can and can't do in the ghetto.

She might hesitate, but she's scared because you're a ghetto cop. No Long Island cop in Smithtown, Hempstead, or Massapequa has ever talked to her like that before. What's more, there are Black and

Hispanic people here. Mercy. So she puts the car in gear and drives off.

And just like clockwork, five minutes later she's back looking for her boyfriend.

Then you pull up on her again. Now the whole situation is turning into a nightmare for her.

"Get out of the fucking car!" you scream at her.

She may or may not be crying or begging just to let her go again.

"I told you not to come back here!" you say. "Now empty your purse, and I swear, if I find a fingernail file, I'm gonna lock you up for a weapons possession!" If you're not familiar with the city and Long Island, then you should know that the odds of *not* finding a fingernail file, or a can of hairspray for that matter, on a Long Island girl, are roughly the same as winning the lottery. Twice. Nails and hair are both big on Long Island.

You just know what's echoing through her head. She's saying to herself, "Oh fuck, why would my boyfriend bring me here?" Which creates an awkward situation for him later.

Soon you've got the purse contents dumped out on the hood of the car and start going through it. Probably, there's nothing in there. But by now, your partner is in her face yelling, "Slut," "Bitch," "Whore," and patting her down. Now, she's being touched in public, humiliated. Usually, there's a group of five or six dealers, steerers, and lookouts standing on the corner, and they're laughing their asses off. And the boyfriend, he's probably still hanging back, wondering where the nearest subway station might be, and if he'll survive the walk.

Now, you order her to put her shit back in the bag and throw it in the car. Then you tell her to, "Get your tight little Long Island white ass back in the car and get the fuck out of here! Or I swear, I swear to Christ, I'll throw your ass in a cell with one of those mutts and he'll rape your ass all night!"

You watch her drive away and call for another car to follow her out. As for the boyfriend: he's stuck. Fuck his stuck. He came into the ghetto to buy drugs. So fuck him.

One night on a slow tour, my partner and I were sitting in the shadows parked behind a van facing south, just bullshitting, when we saw this white Monte Carlo pull up. The driver pulled onto a one-way road that goes north.

As we watched, a white guy got out of the car to do his deal, car running, leaving the girlfriend behind in the passenger seat.

So we called for backup, and while we're waiting, he returned, got in his car, and pulled away. Just then, the other RMP pulled up behind him as he came to a stop sign. At this point his full attention was behind him, focused on the cops in his rearview mirror. And suddenly, everything became legal—the full stop at the stop sign, the right turn signal, everything. He probably hadn't followed all the driving laws since he took his road test, but now, in the ghetto, at three in the morning, with the NYPD right behind him, he's driving like everyone's grandmother. It's what my father used to call "instant religion."

Just as he started pulling away, we came out from behind the shadows, hitting the high beams, turret lights, and spot lights. The RMP behind him did the same thing.

Our car doors flew open, and, with our guns drawn, we bum rushed the car. "Don't fucking move! Put the car in park!" Just like on TV.

At this point, you know they're shitting bricks, especially the girl.

He's got cops behind him, cops in front of him, and bright lights in his eyes. He's probably in a total fucking panic. Cops are yelling and pointing guns at him. But for us, it's like role playing; something to do on a slow night.

A couple of cops came up from behind and opened the doors to his car. They pulled the pair out and put them on the hood. I noticed the girl first. She wasn't bad looking, maybe 19 or 20. Dark, shoulder-length hair, tassled boots, and a leather jacket. The guy had dark hair, a mustache, a leather jacket, and he was shaking like a leaf. Basically, he looked like a loser. Just some kid who works in a mall and didn't know what he was going to do with his life. Everything about him said, "All I have is my babe, my crack, and my Monte Carlo—and I can barely afford all three."

We frisked him, "What's this bulge? Is this a gun?"

"No, no man, it's a pack of cigarettes," he answered, nervous and trying to collect himself.

"Don't lie to me! Don't you fucking lie to me! I'll beat the fucking piss out of you!"

"Cigarettes man, really, really, please."

And he was looking at his girlfriend across the car's hood. I saw everything in that look; it said, "Oh man, I'm going to jail. Help!"

I glanced back and saw a couple of the other guys tossing the car. Totally trashing it. And I knew that someone was going to find their way to the fuse box and pull a couple of the fuses, so it would take forever to find out what was wrong with the lights, blinkers, or stereo.

Meanwhile, I'm saying, "Where is it? Where the fuck is it?"

We didn't find any drugs on this particular guy. The dealer's spotter saw us and turned him away.

The drug dealer's crew were grouped in a loose knot on the corner, yucking it up. Dissing the white boy from a safe distance. The message to the white kid is: Now, how do you like dealing with the man like *you* were some ghetto nigger? How do you like being dissed out in the street?

"Don't you know when you pull up here, don't you know that these motherfuckers are going to rob you?

Take your car. Butt fuck your girlfriend? Don't you fucking know that?"

By now, the guy's wimpering on the hood while a couple more cops tear his car apart.

"Don't you know they'll turn your girlfriend into a cheap whore? Rip her ass apart?" Then to the girl, "Did you know that? Every one of those mutts'll fuck you till you bleed."

From somewhere she found some courage. Trying to take control of the situation and establish that she's different from whatever other type of person we may be used to dealing with, she said, "You don't have to talk to me like that officer."

"Oh, excuse me, yes I do," I answered. "Because that's exactly what's going to happen." I grabbed her by the forearm and started walking her to the corner. "Yo, money, c'mere man! You want a fresh piece of ass! I got a fresh piece of pussy right here!"

Of course nobody on the corner moved, but by now they're bent over with laughter. This is great street theater for them. A couple of white kids being tossed by the man.

After half a dozen steps, she started to cry.

"Don't cry like a fucking baby," I said. "If you're woman enough to come in here to buy drugs, you're woman enough to deal with the whole thing."

"Officer, I promise, I promise," she cried. "I'll never come back. I promise, please. I'll do anything."

So I walked her back to the car, where the boyfriend was still on the hood. One of the other cops had pulled out a sterile surgeon's glove we use when we search perps. He's rolled up his shirt sleeve and is snapping the glove up his forearm like Ben Casey.

Looking over his shoulder, the kid's eyes grew wider and wider with fear. Nobody's said anything, but it was clear that this cop intended to do a "full cavity" search out on the street.

By now I'm beginning to envy the guys on the corner, because they're able to laugh. Along with the other cops, I'm having a hard time keeping a straight face. The whole scene had digressed into the sick and sadistic. I knew it then, even trying to keep from laughing, and I know it now, when it hardly seems funny. But now I recognize it for what it was—a sick humor in drawing fear from a helpless person.

The whole thing dissolved after that. I brought the kid up off the hood so he was facing me and started talking to both of them. "How would you feel if those five niggers over there fucked your girlfriend and made you watch? Then fucked you in the ass. Then shot and stabbed her. Or shot and stabbed you. All because your cheap little Long Island white ass wants to come into *my precinct* to buy drugs." The message is: I belong here. Those mutts on the corner, they belong here. You, you fucking don't belong here.

Silence from the two.

"You two, you're fucking pathetic. Now get the fuck out of here."

They drove off a short time later. If they'd gotten lippy or insulting, we could have disconned them, wrote them a summons, and held them for four hours. But instead, we had another car follow them out of the area.

We turned off the turret lights and drove around the block to the other side of Crescent and Pine streets. Now we were going to pinch the corner where the dealers were, by bum rushing it in the same way.

Two cars came up from different angles with the lights out. One car came up Pitkin from Pine, and the other came down Crescent, heading down both streets the wrong way.

Both cars moved slowly and quietly to the corner, until finally, at about thirty yards away, one of the lookouts spotted us. And boom, we hit the corner. Lights on, out of the car, guns drawn. A couple of the guys tried to run, but we caught them and herded them back into the group.

"Okay, up on the wall!"

"Take that fucking hat off," someone yelled and threw the guy's hat on the ground.

"Yo man, why you got to do that to my rim?"

"Shut the fuck up," someone said, and smacked him across the back of the head.

This wasn't acting, this was for real.

"Yo, that fucking white boy just gave you up," one of the cops said.

"What the fuck you mean?"

"Fucking white boy, he gave you up. Don't give me 'what the fuck you mean?' You know what you're fucking doing here."

"Yo, officer, we're just hangin' man."

"You had your laugh when we were tossing the white boy. But he gave you up. Now be a fucking man and take it. And we'll be on our way."

There's no fear here from these guys. This is just a fucking inconvenience for them. Every second we're on the corner, they're losing money. And they resent us for it.

I tossed the nearby garbage can looking for their stash. Someone else was searching them. A cop found a stem (glass crack pipe) and crushed it. Another cop kicked their "boom box" off a milk crate, cracking the case.

"Yo man, why you gotta do that?"

" 'Cause you can buy another one. Cause you can afford a hundred of 'em. Now shut the fuck up and stay on the wall."

After a little while, we took everyone's pedigree (name, address, etc.). As they all squared themselves away, we got them in a little group.

"Here's the deal," I said. "I don't want you fucking guys hanging around here anymore. I pull up, you're gone. I shouldn't have to get out of the fucking car. I get out of my car and toss you again, and again, and again. And if I do it enough, if I lose my patience, I'm gonna lock you up. I'll own your ass for four hours. I'll take four hours from your life, cause I got all the time in the world. Eight and a half hours, I can do anything with it. And I still get paid. I'm gonna take you off the street and for four hours you won't get paid."

"Yo man, we got it," one of them said, while another chimed in, "Yo, hear it."

And you know they did. So I eased off into a joke. "Man, what you selling to white people for? You know they give you up?"

A couple of heads nodded in agreement.

"Man, white people, they don't want to go to jail. They'll give you up in a heartbeat."

More nods.

"Now, step off in the direction you live," I said. "Not into the store down the street. Go home."

They walked off, but ten minutes later, after we'd left, they'd be back and open for business.

The point of the whole incident is that you have to establish one fact: that you control everything. You just controlled the white boy from Long Island, which was observed by the street, and you just as equally controlled them.

If they had all stepped off right after we had tossed the kid from Long Island, it would have been, "Sorry you had to miss the show, but you owe me that respect." Everybody's got to make money. Everybody's got to do their job. For those guys on the corner, it's an economic fact that they have to deal drugs. It's a choice between asking, "Will that be a large Coke with that hamburger?" for minimum wage at Burger King or standing on a corner for a couple hundred bucks a night dealing drugs. That isn't even a choice. But when I come around, show some respect. You step off and let me do my job. At least show me that much.

But the thing that really gets me about these kids who come into the ghetto to buy their drugs is how many of them have a father, or cousin, or uncle who's either a cop or a detective. They're holding a PBA (police union) card with a shield number on it and will give up who they know "on the job," in a flash. That's embarrassing. So I tell them, "How would you feel if I woke them up, right now, and told them I was holding you here? Told them that you admitted you were buying drugs and you gave them right up? Just because you fucking know someone on the job, that doesn't make it okay to come here and buy drugs."

The saddest thing, which I never say, is that even though I don't know who their friend or relative is on the job, I'm embarrassed, deeply and genuinely. But they'll never know it.

The other thing is, the dealers on the corner probably won't rob or kill the kid who comes in from Long Island to buy his drugs. It's bad for business. When word gets out, "Hey you can't go to that location anymore, because they rob white people," that hurts sales. Sometimes they'll rip them off after the fact, by having another guy rob them of the drugs they just bought and whatever money's left in their pockets. But even that's self-defeating. The first principle of good business, even in the ghetto, is that it's safe to buy here. There's still an element of fear; there has to be. It keeps the outsiders in line. Those white kids don't belong there. The dealers don't talk to them nicely. It's: "Yo man, ten bucks, give me the fucking money!" It's a quick hand-to-hand transaction and a done deal. After which, both players go their own way; each thinking the other is pathetic.

What it is, truthfully, is business.

And that's all it is.

As graduation approached, my mother and father grew more anxious about my future. There were a couple of questions about what I intended to do with my life, but I ducked them nicely.

Maybe they figured I hadn't made up my mind yet. But the trouble was, I had made up my mind. I wanted to be a cop.

It was around February or March when I heard about the Provincetown, Massachusetts "Specials." Provincetown, or P-town, as it's called, hired part-time cops for the summer months.

P-town is an old New England town on the ocean. It's where the Pilgrims first touched down as winter approached; but they didn't like the scenery and moved on to Plymouth. The problem, of course, was that they arrived after summer had ended.

Years ago, it was an artists colony where the local Yankees tolerated the writers, painters, actors, and musicians because they spent freely. Their antics were also probably a cheap source of entertainment. Eugene O'Neill, Edna St. Vincent Millay, and Clifford Odets all spent time there. The loose troupe first performed their plays at a wharf theater in P-town, before coming to New York's Greenwich Village.

Today, P-town is still a tolerant place. A summer haven for gay people, it's very upscale and quaint, with the same kind of comfortable "authentic" charm as Aspen. The restaurants stock vintage wines and there is an abundance of art galleries and designer clothing boutiques.

There is an ancient P-town joke in which a young lady from New York City sees a local fisherman in yellow rain gear walking down the docks. "There sure are a lot of colorful people here," she says to a local merchant. "Sure is, but after Labor Day they'll all be gone," he replied.

The "Specials" took a month-long training course with the state police, then were assigned jobs in Provincetown. It was understood that the jobs were strictly summer employment to handle the overflow crowds during the tourist season. During the slow winter months, the dozen full-time cops were all that was needed for patrol. This arrangement saved the taxpayers money and provided trained police protection.

I sent in my application and was accepted immediately.

When spring break came, I spent the week lounging around my folks' summer house on Cape Cod. It's a big place, on a semi-private street two minutes from the ocean, and the town has something of a nightlife. I threw myself into partying and enjoying spring break, but never mentioned P-town.

The way I figured it, I could work as a cop in P-town and commute the fifty miles or so from my parents' summer house. The summer would be like a test, to see if I liked being a cop and if I was any good at it.

Throughout spring break, the question hung there, unasked, unanswered, and avoided. "What are you going to do with your life?"

By the end of the week, my parents headed back to Shaker and I headed back to school. A few weeks into the semester, the question was no longer being ignored. Not a phone call or a visit went by when they didn't ask about my plans for the future.

Sometime around late April, with graduation only a few weeks away, my mother called. I had just received my training instructions in the mail and was more than a little excited about the job. "I'm going to be working in P-town as a Special this summer," I said, blurting it all out at once.

"A special what?" she asked, suspicious. I knew that P-town part didn't sound good.

"A cop! I'm going to be a cop this summer!"

The pause on the other end of the phone was so long that I thought the line had gone dead. Finally she spoke. "Oh," my mother said.

Personally, I thought she took it quite well.

7

IT'S THE daily stuff that grinds you down in police work. I didn't plan on saving the world when I became a cop, even a kid from the suburbs isn't that naive. But I did want to save a piece of it. That isn't naive, that's arrogant. I thought maybe I could help people. They would come to me or I would go to them, and when I left, they would be better off. Their lives would be better.

How this would happen, I didn't know. I have to confess, I didn't have a fucking clue. Maybe somewhere along the way, in the Police Academy, from a partner, or on the street, I'd learn the secret. I'd learn to speak the lines that would make it all right. A lot of cops feel that way, but when it doesn't happen and you realize it never will happen—it can't happen—that's when the work becomes a battle you know you can't win. It grinds you to dust.

Domestic disputes are the perfect example of no-win situations. This is the way they start: Most of them stem directly from alcohol. And most of them happen late at night or first thing in the morning. A husband or wife comes home later than expected. Questions are raised about where they were until midnight or three in the morning. And no answers are being offered, just a lot of hemming and hawing. Suspicion grows, and the decibel level jumps. A little while later, the swinging starts. And when the swinging starts, weapons suddenly appear. A baseball bat, a kitchen knife, a broken jar, or a gun. And then the police are called.

Frequently, it's a child, a three, four, or five year old, who makes the call. The kid might be laying under the covers in his or her bed in the middle of the night, scared to death because of the screaming and fighting.

If it's not a kid, then it's a neighbor, or whoever is getting the worst from the fight. Frequently the phone is disconnected, yanked from the wall by the aggressor and used as a weapon. So, by the time you hear about it, you're only getting half the story from the dispatcher who maybe only got half the story herself before getting cut off.

You can watch the cops on TV, on those "real-life" cop shows, and they've got all the compassion in the world. I could script an hour's worth of compassion too, with the cameras rolling. But after you show up at two or three hundred of these things, how much compassion can you have left.

A lot of the cops now, they don't even get out of their cars, especially in the winter. Their attitude is *you called me, so you come out to my car in this freezing weather*. It's like that for most of the Brooklyn North precincts. It's what you would call a real trend. The cop will radio the dispatcher and have her do a "callback," telling the complainants to meet you at the curb. A lot of cops don't even turn off the RMP's engine. I'm guilty of this, I'll admit it, though most cops won't. I've turned to my partner and sneered, "NYPD Complaint Window, may I help you?" as a complainant approached the car.

Worse still, if there isn't a callback number, the cop will double-tap the RMP's horn, "wooping" the siren. If no one responds, they'll leave and make the job a "90X," non-existent complainant.

But when the cops do show up and get out of their car, a lot of times the woman will get behind the near-est cop and start swinging her arms over his shoulders and yelling, "Come on, come on through the cop to get at me!" She'll just start antagonizing the shit out of the guy.

A typical case happened a couple of years ago. We pulled up to this house, and a guy came out and said nothing was going on. I said, "Go get your wife. I want her to tell me that, because she's the one who called."

So the guy goes back inside and grabs this woman by the arm and starts dragging her out the door. She's fighting tooth and nail as he drags her out. Maybe she didn't want to talk to the cops or maybe she just didn't want to go out in the cold.

Anyway, he was about halfway to the curb when she started swinging at him. And he started slapping the shit out of her.

I looked over at my partner and it was written all over his face. We were thinking the same thing: "What a fucking nightmare." So we got out of the car to separate them.

"Okay, what's going on here?" my partner asked.

Now that we were closer, I could smell the alcohol. Both of them were plastered.

"He hit me," she said.

And the guy said, "She hit me!"

"Goddamned right I hit you!" she answered, and tried to hit him again.

Now we have cross complainants. Two drunk people bitch-slapping each other. These people were in their mid-forties, and here we were, two cops—my partner is 26 and I'm 28—acting like referees.

At this point, as far as I was concerned, it's a matter of two X's equalling an 0. We've got nothing and there's nothing we could do about it. All we could do is ask the guy to spend the night somewhere else. But if he doesn't want to, we can't make him leave. It's his house.

Suddenly the woman, disgusted with us, ran back into the house while we were talking to the guy. She came out a minute later, and started all over again.

"I don't fucking want you two! I want two other cops. The dispatcher told me to get your names and badge numbers," she said. She'd dialed 911 again and told them she didn't like the way we were handling the situation.

"So get it," I said.

"Give me your pen!"

"What? Give you *my* pen? Let you use my pen to make a complaint against me? Get the fuck out of here."

"That's exactly what I'm gonna do. When I'm laying dead in the gutter, I'm gonna sue your ass."

"How you gonna do that, if you're dead?"

"My family's gonna sue."

"Can't sue, you don't have my name or badge number."

And she started cursing me out.

"Lady, you're drunk," I said. Then I got back on the radio and said, "5-10." Abbreviated radio talk for "75-Sp10" that identifies our car to central.

I guess the woman heard wrong, because she started screaming, mimicking me, "5-len! 5-len," over my shoulder:

The dispatcher came back, "5-10."

"Yeah, this is gonna be a 90Y, 'pparently intox," I said, 10-90Y is the code for an unnecessary call.

Then the lady started screaming, "Intox! Intox! Fucking right, I'm intoxed!"

When I let go of the transmission button, the dispatcher came back chuckling, "Apparently so."

Toward the end, when I saw the hopelessness of it was just overwhelming, I asked, "Does he work?"

And the woman said, "Hell no!"

"Do you work?"

"No."

"Lady, what good reason do you have for being up at four in the morning on a Monday night arguing like this?" I asked, almost pleading. "If you're waking up for work, that's one thing, but lady, it's four in the fucking morning! Can you give me a reason? Enlighten me, please. Give me some form of logic behind this madness."

And, like always, it's "we were out drinking all night." It's almost always drinking—but what triggered the dispute could have been anything trivial. It might just as easily have been "he was out drinking all night."

They settled down after that, so my partner and I got back in the car. As soon as I put the car in gear to pull away from the curb, she'd positioned herself right behind the RMP. She's screaming again, "Run me over! Motherfucker, run me over so I can sue your ass!"

The husband dragged her back and said, "Shut up, can't you see he's trying to help you." And he smacked her across the face.

She broke away from him and started off down the street, screaming. It's four in the morning and she's screaming bloody murder at the top of her lungs. The guy, he just stood there for a moment, shook his head, then walked back into the house.

I'm sure domestic disputes happen in Shaker too. I've never been a cop there, but I can picture it. Spouses probably fight about the same things: money and pussy, too many questions asked and not enough answers being offered. You can picture the officer coming to the door, and the vice president of some bank greeting him by saying, "It's nothing officer, you know how women are."

"Yep, got one myself," the cop would say with a grim nod and a slight smile.

"Thanks then, officer," the guy says, hoping that none of his neighbors saw the police car in front of his house. "See you at Christmas time."

A few days later, the couple may be sitting in a nice mahogany-paneled office talking to a marriage counselor. Or, she's explaining away the black eye to friends by saying she had an accident on the tennis courts. Or, she's sitting in a lawyer's office by herself planning how she can keep the house, the cars, and the stock portfolio.

*   *   *

After I'd been in the 7-5 a few months, my father went out on tour with me and we got a call for a domestic dispute. The place was at the north end of the precinct, in a fairly decent neighborhood filled with hardworking people. When we got to the house, it looked pretty well-maintained.

We went to the door and a guy let us in. I sized up the situation immediately. They were an older couple, both in their late forties or early fifties. And immediately, the woman started off with her story; something about him coming home late with no explanation, and how this shit happens all the time and she won't put up with it any more.

But, the guy never raised a hand to her. No crime had been committed. It wasn't a police matter, it was a personal matter.

My partner was in the other room, trying to get the story from the lady. There was a little kid, maybe seven or eight, sitting on the couch watching TV. His eyes kept going from us to the TV and then back to us—like he couldn't make up his mind what was more interesting.

I was in the entranceway talking to the guy, who seemed reasonable, my dad at my side. But you could see that if we just left, the thing would escalate into something ugly. So I said to the guy, "Look, things don't seem to be working out here. Maybe it'd be a good idea if you split, before it gets any worse."

The guy nodded his head, agreeing. Now this was his house. He hadn't committed a crime. He could've told me to go fuck myself, and he'd be in the right. After all, who the fuck am I to come into someone's house and suggest they leave in the middle of the night? But I guess he saw the logic in it, because his wife was showing no signs of winding down.

So the guy went upstairs to get his jacket while I waited in the hallway, trying to maintain eye contact with my partner.

"Aren't you going to watch that guy?" my father asked.

I kind of gave him a look and said, "No, he went up to get his jacket. What concern is that of mine?"

Suddenly, my father started tapping me on the shoulder. "He's coming down!" my father whispered. "Here he comes!"

"Great," I said. "Now, quit bugging me about it."

The guy came back down with his jacket, and the wife was still ranting. The guy was on his way out, so that should have ended the discussion. But she's still on him and I'm thinking, if this guy beat the shit out of her, he'd have good reason. I'd have locked him up. But he would have sat in the back of my RMP in handcuffs and said, "Man, she drove me to this."

I would have agreed with him too, saying, "I believe you, one hundred percent."

But the guy left, and we got back in the car and pulled away. And as soon as we moved, my father said, "Doesn't that bother you?"

"What? Doesn't what bother me?"

"You let that guy out of your sight," my father said. "He could have gone and got a shotgun."

"What if he had? I would have shot him first. But he wasn't getting a shotgun, he was getting his jacket."

"What gives you the confidence in that?"

"Because you can tell by people's motions. He wasn't hyped up or running up the stairs. The guy just wanted to get out of the house. When he goes back the next day, he can tell his wife the cops told him to leave."

To this day, I don't know why my father put so much emphasis on that. The things I worry about are "gun runs," drug locations, or abandoned crack houses that are booby-trapped. Those things make me more nervous than a domestic dispute.

If anything, disputes are an inconvenience more than a threat. If you're poor, there are no mahogany-paneled offices available to sit in and talk things out with a marriage counselor. There are no lawyers to call who will ease the wife into a comfortable life. For these people, there is only the bored cop and the back of an RMP.

Once I showed up at a run-down house at three in the morning. It looked as if it was being renovated. There was sheet plastic over the windows, and inside, the place was in disarray. There wasn't much heat, either. We were inside, but I was freezing, even in my duty jacket, sweater, and turtleneck.

The grandmother had called us. "Officer, I have to go to work in two hours and I have a little girl, a little boy, and an infant crying," she said. "And I don't know where the mother is."

"Who's the mother?" I asked.

"My daughter."

"How old are the children?"

"Seven, five, and eight months."

A little girl came down the stairs, fully dressed and sleepy eyed. I walked over to her, "Hi dear, how you doing? Where's your mommy?"

"I don't know, she left with some man."

"Your father?"

"No."

"Did he drag her out?"

"No."

"Do you know where she might be going?"

"Up the street somewhere."

So, we were there for an hour and a half. The grandmother worked for a city agency, and the clock was ticking toward the time when she had to get on the subway. You knew she needed the job. It fed and clothed the kids and paid for the house. Who knows how many times she'd missed work in the past because of her daughter. She probably didn't know who else to call, so she called the cops.

We kept going 'round and 'round on the options. There were only three of them: We or she could call BCW (Bureau of Child Welfare); she could miss work waiting for the mother to come home; or we could file a complaint for abandonment and lock up the mother, which, in the long run, forces us to apply options one and two. Absolutely a no-win situation.

If we called the BCW, the kids would lose everything—meaning the mother, for those times she's around, the grandmother, and each other. The kids would more than likely be placed in different foster homes and then bounced around from one place to another for years. A lot of foster parents who sponsor kids treat the situation as a business. They get a few hundred bucks a month per child, then try to turn a profit on the deal.

But those were the immediate choices we had in front of us. There just weren't any others.

The mother finally came in the door at the last possible minute. Years of drug abuse showed on her thin face. Maybe I was hoping against the odds for something better to come through the door. Someone with a legit excuse that would signal that the kids would be okay and this wouldn't happen again. But I looked at the acne scars and sunken eyes, and knew it would happen again. She smelled like bitter smoke, like crack, and there was a hint of liquor on her breath.

As for the grandmother, she was already rushing out the door, scared to death she was going to be late for a job that kept them out of a shelter.

My partner and I started to ream the mother out good. Really dumping on her, guilt, threats, everything we could think of—but it just went in one ear and out the other. We'd been freezing in that house and sweating out the choices, busting our brains for an hour and a half, trying to think of ways of keeping the kids—*her kids*—out of the system, and for her it was just another day-in-the-life.

Don't expect niceties from me about it. This one really got to me *because* of the grandmother and the kids. They were the only reasons for us taking the time to partially resolve this dilemma. As for the mother, fuck her, she was beyond help. She was out getting high, drunk, and probably fucked. Maybe whoring herself off in a crack house or spending money that the kids needed for clothes and food on her habit.

You see, you show up at a domestic dispute not knowing what the stories are going to be. You don't want to hear the whole story, which may very well take an hour or more to hear and understand. Inevitably someone says, "You don't care."

They're right, I don't care. Not any more. I have cared and cared and cared. I have talked and cajoled, given out numbers, and used every trick I could think up. I have opened veins—expended my compassion, sympathy, and pity on strangers. And in return, I've been attacked, threatened, and cursed. Women, still bleeding from the wounds their husbands inflicted on them, have jumped on my back trying to kill me as I handcuffed the asshole who beat them bloody.

In the end, I was faced with the question, why should I care? I'm not related to you. I'm not your son, your husband, your mother, or your father. I'm a cop. More than likely the only reason I'm here, in your home, is because you were disturbing your neighbors by beating up on each other. It's a crime to beat up another person, and someone called me because a crime was being committed.

And they'll say, "Why don't you have some decency and compassion?"

It's not my job to have those things. It's my job to keep some guy from beating up his wife. If I have to lock him up to do it, then that's what I'll do. What else can I do? The whole thing is a trap. If you care for one, you have to care for a thousand. After that thousand, there's ten thousand more. And ten thousand after that. I just don't have that kind of energy. Nobody does.

I've shown up at innumerable domestic disputes where a woman had a bloody lip and a bump on her head the size of an egg. And I've asked them, flat out, "Do you want him locked up?"

The answer I usually get is, "No, I don't want him locked up. I just want him out of here."

Well, I'm not a city marshall. By law, I don't have the authority to evict people from their homes. All I can do is ask the guy to leave on his own, but if he says, "I ain't leaving," then there's nothing I can do. The guy lives there, he has a right to be there.

Most of the time the women just want the guy gone, temporarily. Ninety-nine times out of a hundred, the guy is still there when we leave. And you know something? If that guy kills her in a half hour, the woman's last words will be, "Fuck that asshole cop!"

All I can do is take a complaint and give her a referral number. But referrals only work if you follow up on them, and few people do. And do I blame them? Fuck yes, I blame them. But do I blame them? No, I can't because I've been down to some of the city's social service agencies. I've seen the lines. Lines that snake and coil back on themselves to cover every square foot of a huge waiting room. Finally, when you reach the end of that line, what's waiting for you isn't a solution or magic potion, but a burned-out caseworker with more numbers and more referrals to more lines at more city agencies.

We'd like to believe we're great providers, protecting battered women, but our protection only lasts as long as the cop is standing in their livingrooms or as long as it takes to get from the back of the line to the front. Because when they leave those lines and the government buildings, sooner or later they have to go home. And what's waiting for them? He is. And he'll probably convince her he won't do it again . . . but he will.

I can picture the police brass reading this and thinking I'm insensitive . . . that it's a negative view of cops. But it isn't, it's a human view of cops. We're not a magic potion that's going to make it—whatever the problem is—go away. The mayor has no magic potion, and neither does One Police Plaza.

There is no magic solution; there are no numbers to call.

8

NINETY-NINE percent of the time, you bust some guy then never hear about it again. You make the arrest, do all the paperwork, meet with the ADAs assigned to the case, and the perps vanish into the system. They go to jail or are back out on the street on probation. Most cases are plea-bargained, out and gone. Very few cops, unless it's an exceptional case, follow it to the final disposition. After awhile, all the faces blur together, and you can't put a name with a section of the penal code.

I've run into guys on the street in downtown Brooklyn, and they'll say, "Yo, Poss!"

When I turn, I'm looking into an unfamiliar face. "I know you, pal?" I'll ask.

"You don't remember me?" the guy will ask back. "Man, you busted me, remember? GLA (grand larceny auto), that's how we met."

That's how "we met"? This guy's talking like we became friends. Like now we should go around the corner to Callahan's Pub, grab a cold one, and catch up on old times. The funny thing is, they're not all that pissed-off about me busting them, but more put out because I don't remember their names. Sorry, but you were one lousy arrest, maybe six hours of OT for me. That's all you were, a body I threw into the system and was duly rewarded for on my paycheck.

75

The best collar I ever had—from chase, arrest, trial, and conviction—came out of nowhere.

I was on the job a few years and working the four-to-midnight shift with Bobby, this big burly cop in his 30s. He was a family man, two kids, a wife, and a house on Long Island—the whole bit. He was ex-military. A heavy-duty weight-lifter, he was buffed out and didn't take shit from anyone.

Even though he was the senior man, I drove that night. It was early summer, and I remembered hearing that a couple of guys in a stolen Pathfinder had done a gas station robbery in Queens, or near the border of Queens and the 7-5. The Queens cops were holding a customized four-wheel-drive vehicle as a "possible" for prints (fingerprints) that was stolen out of the 7-3, our sister precinct in Brownsville.

We were in sector E-F (Eddie-Frank), heading north down Snediker Avenue towards New Lots Avenue, when I spotted a blue Mustang convertible with the top up. The male driver was parked at the curb on New Lots, facing East. The car was packed with people, and music with a very heavy bass was coming from inside.

We passed by them, made the right onto New Lots, and as we were turning, I looked in the rearview mirror and saw them leave. We went five blocks down, made a left, and went a couple of blocks up. That put us westbound on Lavonia Avenue, a main street shadowed by L tracks with stores, vacant lots, decaying tenements, and warehouses on either side.

On the top two storys of one building—an old factory or warehouse—you can still see the billboard-sized sign advertising Fortunoff's original store painted across the weather-worn brick. It's a genuine urban antique. The paint, old beyond flaking but soaked into the brick, now advertises nothing but the fact that the neighborhood had a more prosperous past, or at least one with some opportunity in the future. In the warmer months, the large double doors of the downstairs open, and someone makes a few bucks selling used furniture on the sidewalk.

But as we turned the corner, we saw the blue Mustang convertible again, coming towards us. I noticed the guy's lights were off, so I blinked my high/lows at him, signaling him to turn his headlights on.

But he didn't do anything.

So I turned the turret lights on.

As soon as I hit the turrets, the guy took a fast right, and rabbits (sped away).

"Maybe this guy's dirty, huh?" I asked my partner.

"Chase him," Bobby said.

We had one of the old Chevies, a 4.3, but it happened to be in great shape. When I punched the gas, the car jumped forward. Some of the cars are so beat to shit that when you punch the gas, they'll spit, sputter, and kick. But, by chance, this was a good car, and we started closing the distance between us and the Mustang.

The guy sped up and made another turn, then another onto Riverdale Avenue towards Pennsylvania Avenue, and another, serpentining down side streets, trying to lose us. We were maybe half a block behind with lights 'n sirens going. When the traffic light turned red, he didn't even slow down.

"Look at that asshole. Definitely stolen," Bobby said. Nobody with that kind of phat (customized expensive) car risks smashing it up by running lights, especially filled with that many people. The rear window of the Mustang was unzipped, and every time I got close enough I could see hands waving out and caught glimpses of faces in the strobe of our turret lights.

"Definitely," I echoed, my concentration glued to the Mustang. All I could think about was, "catch, catch, catch."

As if to prove us right, the guy blew through red lights left and right, weaving in and out of traffic. Soon we approached Pennsylvania Avenue, a major thoroughfare, and still hadn't put the chase over the radio.

There's an unspoken, actually frequently spoken, rule that you don't put high-speed pursuits over the radio. Just the mention of the word "pursuit" implies speed, the chance of civilians being injured, and the eventuality of multi-million-dollar lawsuits against the city and the department. You'll also get a lot of questions from the dispatcher and other units, adding to the chaos in a situation that demands concentration. And, the fucking instant you put the pursuit over, the sergeant will "call it off." If you mention it at all, you keep your voice dead calm and use words like "following" or "observing." If the sergeant hears the smallest trace, the slightest inflection of excitement in your voice, he'll end it. The trick is to make going eighty miles an hour the wrong way down a pot-holed, one-way, side street sound like a six mile an hour driver's education spin in a high school parking lot.

At Pennsylvania Avenue and Linden Boulevard, he saw a break in traffic and made a sharp right, cutting through a self-service gas station at fifty miles an hour. I followed him through the station and onto a service road that parallels Linden Boulevard; a multi-lane road that goes from one end of Brooklyn to the other and cuts into Queens. The boulevard's divided by a concrete island, and lined with light poles and fast-food restaurants.

I glanced over and saw Bobby white-knuckling the dash, probably debating if this whole chase thing was such a good idea.

Up ahead some cars were stopped at a light, and the Mustang cut off two, then zoomed through the intersection and turned onto Linden Boulevard. But I couldn't get through the intersection. My lights and sirens were going, but nobody moved. They were like deer caught in headlights.

Finally we got them out of the way and hit Linden Boulevard. Up ahead was an ESU truck, the one cops call "the big truck," which carries specialized equipment: guns, helmets, and rescue gear. We passed them like they were standing still.

At this point, we were right on the border between the 7-3 and 7-5 precincts. The Mustang had a good lead on us as they approached the border, marked by elevated subway tracks, made a sharp left, then a right. We lost sight of them.

As I rounded the second corner, there they were, sideways on the street. The driver must've lost control on the turn, and was trying to re-start the car. I was going so fast, it looked like we were going to ram them broadside.

As I jammed on the brakes, people started piling out of the car, through the rear window and the doors, like a circus clown act. We screeched forward for what seemed like miles, our car coming to a stop inches from their passenger door, blocking it.

Both of us jumped out. We had our guns drawn and started chasing a couple of the perps across Linden Boulevard. I went after the driver, and he swung at me with a bottle. I swung back as he made a grab for my gun. While I'm trying to re-holster, he started pulling my duty jacket over my head. Then got in a couple of good punches, that knocked me back a couple of steps, before turning to bolt. I fell back, breaking my fall against the car, and a sharp pain shot through my wrist and thumb. I lunged forward from the ground, grabbing his jacket with one hand, but he twisted, slipped out of it, and ran across the boulevard.

Bobby had his guy locked up and on the hood of the car, but my guy got away leaving me holding his coat. Fuck it!

I chased the guy across the boulevard toward Coney Island Joe's, a fast-food restaurant adjacent to a transit storage yard. The yard is where they keep gravel, railroad ties, and equipment. It's a huge place surrounded by razor-wire fencing.

Then the "big truck" came barrelling up. I started

pointing and yelling as they passed one of the perps I was chasing. Just as they passed him, the truck's rear double doors flew open and a cop reached out with one hand and grabbed the guy by the scruff of his collar. The grab threw the guy off balance, and he stumbled once, then half fell as the truck eventually slowed to a stop.

Bobby had one of the perps and ESU had another one. I wanted one. I didn't know what these guys did, except make me chase them, but I definitely wanted one. I started running up the hill to the railyard where I'd seen another suspect go. There was a couple of ESU guys with shotguns running into the yard just a little ahead of me.

The ESU cops reached him before I did. The guy was hung up on a fifteen-foot-high fence topped with razor-wire. They were grabbing him by the feet, trying to pull him back down, the wire tearing the shit out of him.

He was screaming, "Don't pull me, man! Fuck man, don't fucking pull!"

One of the ESU cops said, "If we let you go, you're going to have to free yourself and climb back down."

"Yeah, man, anything, just don't fucking pull!"

So the ESU guys let him go.

Two seconds later, he managed to climb over to the other side. But there was another fence two feet beyond the first one. The two fences formed a narrow alley, like a dog run, and the guy started running, looking for a way out of the railyard.

By now, it's turned into Keystone cops. There's a perp running back and forth between the two fences. The three or four ESU guys with shotguns were chasing him from the other side of the fence, and I'm chasing him with my service revolver out.

Finally, after a minute or two of this idiocy, we've all had enough. One of the ESU cops said, "Look, we got you asshole, no matter what! If you make us cut the fucking fence, you're a dead man!"

The perp slowed down a little, thought about it, and stopped. "Okay, man, I'm coming back over."

"Fucking better make it quick," one of the ESU cops snapped.

The guy climbed up the fence, then gingerly started to straddle the razor wire. As soon as he got a foot over, one of the ESU guys jumped up, grabbed his foot and yanked him down, just cutting the shit out of him some more.

When the guy hit the ground, the ESU cops shouldered me out of the way and gave him a few good body blows with their shotgun butts before putting the cuffs on. Surprisingly, nobody asked me what he had done.

Now we've got three guys and a Mustang convertible. But we're still trying to figure out what the fuck these guys did. Then a 7-3 car drives by and sees the commotion. A second later, he went over the radio, asking if anything was going on, maybe even something he should know about? Who could blame him, there was a fuck of a lot of blue uniforms around, not to mention the "big truck." So I got back on the portable and told him what we had.

When we all got back to the Mustang, I noticed a gun half-wedged down between the center console and the passenger seat. It was a MAC-11. One of the ESU guys picked it up and tried to clear the chamber. "Fuck, look at this," he said, holding it out. "It's jammed."

When I looked over, I saw him trying to clear two rounds from the chamber; one of them was compressed, the bullet squeezed down into its shell casing.

"I think these guys tried to shoot at you," the ESU cop said.

When he said it, I felt my jaw drop.

Now we have three out of the four, maybe five, guys from the car. We have a gun. And when I looked in the jacket the guy slipped off, there was another fully loaded clip for the MAC-11; a payroll stub, a social security card, and a photo ID card.

My partner called in the plates on the Mustang, and it "came back stolen," taken earlier that day in the 9-0 Precinct, in the Williamsburg section of Brooklyn.

We finally made it back to the precinct, and I was starting on my paperwork when one of the cops from Brooklyn North Task Force mentioned something about a Nissan Pathfinder. The 104th Precinct in Queens, which borders the northern part of the 7-5, called "City Line," was holding it and dusting it for prints. One of the guys we caught had a Nissan car key in his jacket pocket.

"Hey, Bobby," I said, playing Sgt. Joe Friday. "I'll finish the paperwork, why don't you go up 'North' and see if this key fits?"

He figured it was a long shot, but did it anyway just to get out of the paperwork. Half an hour later he came back. Unbelievably, the key fucking fit. Now it was getting complicated.

As I'd found out, the Pathfinder was also stolen and used during a robbery in Queens a few days earlier. And the 1-0-4 didn't want to give up the Pathfinder because it was used in the commission of an armed robbery of a gas station in the 110th precinct, which is also in Queens.

However, the guys we'd pursued and arrested were on the Brooklyn side of the Brooklyn/Queens border. The social security card, payroll stub, and ID belonged to a guy with an address in the 7-5.

As it turned out, these guys were ahead of their time. They'd do a carjacking, rob the occupants, use the car in a robbery at a store, and then do another carjacking. But they kept moving, crossing into different precincts, and bouncing back and forth between Queens, Brooklyn, and Manhattan.

We were just about to take the whole mess before a grand jury and get the three guys indicted when a screw-up occurred. The 180-80 date passed, which means if the suspects don't go before a grand jury within five days after arrest, they get cut lose. I hadn't even given my testimony yet. The scheduled date of the 180-80 was my RDO (regular day off), and nobody called me at home or notified the precinct. Maybe somebody thought it was a nothing case, or maybe they wanted to cut down on cop overtime. But something in the system broke down, and nobody was indicted.

A month later, to the day, a cop from 7-3 RIP (robbery squad) called me up and said, "Hey, Joe, we came into the 7-5 and went up to Ridgewood Avenue and got these four guys, two of them had guns, three we locked up for robbery/GLA (Grand Larceny Auto). They're wanted in Queens, they're wanted in Brooklyn. But there's this fourth guy, I think you might be interested in him. His name's Miguel Oliphant Pena."

"Yeah?" I answered, interested.

A little while later, I found myself doing an ID show-up in the 7-3 RIP office. As I sat down to help with the paperwork, I noticed four guys in the corner handcuffed to chairs. They all looked very familiar. These were the same fucking guys from the car chase. A second later, a DT (detective) hustled me out, saying something about it being a better idea if I waited in the hall or something.

But this time we had other complainants: the guy who owned the Pathfinder, the one who owned the Mustang, his girlfriend, and her friend. They were all in their cars when they were robbed.

The girlfriend and friend were both still pissed off and picked the perps out of the lineups right off the bat. But the male complainants were shakey and too scared to testify. They only wanted their cars back.

I went 'round and 'round with Mr. Mustang, yelling at the guy, but he was too scared. In the end, it was the girlfriend who came through like a champ.

The next grand jury date came around, and everyone showed up to testify: the DTs from Queens and Brooklyn; 7-3 RIP; Mr. Pathfinder; Mr. Mustang and his girlfriends; and me. And we got all four guys indicted.

A year and a half later, after numerous testimonies,

introductions of evidence, and delays, it was still on
hold. Nobody from the DA's office wanted the case.
One ADA kept passing it off to another. It became
infamous as the case nobody wanted. Nobody wanted it
because it was too complicated, and they ran the chance
of losing.

Finally, Vance Carter, an attorney from the Law
Enforcement Investigation Bureau (LEIB), came charg-
ing in just like the calvary. LEIB lawyers try improprieties and criminal misconduct by cops, but in their spare
time pick up criminal cases, like regular ADAs, to keep
in practice.

Vance is a very tall and distinguished black guy. With
his Brooks Brothers suits and professional attitude, he
looks and talks like he should be doing corporate law.
He had a reputation for being tenacious, thorough, and
smart. The judges knew and respected him, so did the
other ADAs. His nickname around the office is "Vance
Romance," which alludes to his suave and gracious manners, but also shows he isn't a burnt-out lawyer.

He actually wanted the case because he'd never handled a felony trial. He saw this case as a way to make his
mark. There was a lot of evidence to be introduced and
a lot of details to be established. And by now, even the
female complainants were getting shakey. Every piece
of preparation in the case was going to have to be
detailed.

I was on the job long enough to have established a
reputation as a very nitpicky cop about paperwork. I
had everything on anybody in this case I'd ever talked
to: phone numbers, pedigrees, vouchers, lab results—
everything. Some cops are careless about how they handle their paperwork. An arrest is just an arrest, OT. But
if it goes to trial, defense attorneys can kill you with
details and paperwork.

So Vance and I got to work. Weekends, days off, and
after work, we'd go over and over the details. We went
out to the scene and took a shitload of Polaroids and

made a big map detailing the route the chase took—through the gas station, traffic lights, where we almost hit pedestrians, where they almost hit pedestrians, where ESU came into play, and where we caught each perp. In the end, they didn't let us use the Polaroids as evidence because the chase took place at dusk, and we shot the pictures during the day. So they were admissable only as "a likeness" of the intersections, railyard, and streets, but not as a "true depiction of the scene at the time of occurrence."

It's unusual for a cop to work with the ADA like that. First off, ADAs don't trust cops all that much. They worry about how cops will act on the stand. Are they going to lie? Did they lie to me? And, are they just fucking stupid? A smart defense attorney can pick away at a cop's story—challenging details, trying to confuse him or her—until nothing's left.

In addition to that, most cops have a distrust for ADAs. We're taught in the academy to be wary of them; they'll try to be your best buddy and get you to say things that may implicate possible misconduct or improprieties. They try to catch cops. They try to indict cops to further their careers.

The department tries to instill in cops that you should cooperate—always cooperate—but never, ever initiate or volunteer anything more than what they ask or require. The rumors and stories about ADAs go on forever. You hear them the same way you hear about some guy inventing a car engine that gets two hundred miles per gallon, but who the oil companies paid off to keep quiet about it. Same type of stories, a cop brought in a felon and ended up doing time himself. A cop brought in a killer, and the ADA refused to prosecute because of a bad search. Always second-, third-, or fourth-hand stories, which are mostly rumored, but largely believed. They're part of cop folklore.

The heart of the conflict is that a cop can fuck up an ADAs case by admission or omission of facts. He could end up helping the perp get off by trying to be too smart for his own good in court, or by being a moron. On the other hand, ADAs can also fuck up, squandering all a cop's hard work that he may have risked his life for by not paying attention to detail, being a bad lawyer, or just getting out-gunned by a better defense attorney. Or worse, by pleading the perp out in some ridiculous legal bargain. And that's a big part of the justice system— Everybody gets a little satisfaction, but no real justice.

Cops think, *"Why should I go out there and risk my life and involve myself in apprehending some felonious asshole, with a multi-faceted crime (recovering guns, drugs, witnesses, and property), if the ADA's just going to plea bargain for a penalty that doesn't fit the crime? Why the fuck should I risk my life for justice that's negotiated like flea-market haggling?"*

There's also conflict between ADAs and cops because of a class thing. ADAs are college and law-school graduates. Many of them are on their way to bigger and better careers as private attorneys. The DA's office is just a stopover, like graduate school. Someplace to get experience.

For cops, all those low-class felonies and petty street arrests are our lives. For the next twenty years, they'll be on special details, on patrol, then taking promotion exams for sergeant, lieutenant, or captain—always working on the career path within the department. A lot of cops are intimidated by even a modicum of intellect.

The whole basis of the car-chase perps' defense was whether there was enough light to see who I was chasing.

The perps were tried in two groups: two guys who were minor players in one group, and Pena and Vargas, the heavy hitters, in another. Both defense attorneys were 118Bs—real lawyers, not public defenders—who put in time doing public defense work.

I hated Pena's lawyer, Eleanor Diggs, immediately.

For one thing, she wore polyester, and for another, she was trying to get this scumbag off with her half-assed, cop-hating attitude. She's renowned for being perpetually pissed off, professionally misplaced, and incompetent in the courtroom.

During the trial, I was drilled numerous times about how, on one of the 61s (complaint report), the suspects' number count of five was whited out and changed to four.

"How do you know it was four suspects and not five?"

"How do you know this is the man you saw that night?"

It went like that for a long time, until finally the judge told Diggs not to bring it up anymore.

But she did manage to knock out my show-up ID that I made at the 7-3. Because Pena told her that I saw him before he went into the lineup room, that tainted the show-up. So we were basically left with no ID, just evidence from a guy who shared the same name as the defendant.

When I took the stand again, the MAC-11 was introduced into evidence, and I pointed it out. I said I saw it in plain view in the front seat of the vehicle with one round in the chamber misfired. Then the loaded clip was introduced as evidence, and I said I found it in the defendant's jacket pocket. Then the payroll stub was introduced, and the name on it is the same as the defendant's. Then the social security card; its number also matching the defendant's. And the picture ID, which also matched the defendant.

The defense lawyer challenged every point. "How do you know this person is the same as my client?"

I answered, "Because when he was arrested, the two social security numbers matched. The one he supplied to the police and the one on the card."

"Well, how do you know he's not using someone else's name and social security number?" she asked.

"Because I also recovered a photo ID that has a picture on it, and that picture is the same likeness as THAT GUY OVER THERE!" And I pointed at Pena.

"Objection! Objection!" Diggs started screaming.

"You can't object to your own line of questioning," the judge countered. "You can only withdraw your questions."

"Your honor, I object to the officer's answer," she shot back.

Suddenly, Vance jumped in, "Your honor, can I recommend that you sustain the officer's answer."

Soon there's a three-way argument between Vance, Diggs, and the judge. Finally, the judge called for a sidebench that included me.

"Officer Poss, don't you remember being instructed not to do an ID?" the judge asked me.

"Yes sir, but how am I supposed to explain my answer to her question without proof?" I asked back. "And besides, he's the one that did it!"

The jury probably heard me, because Vance was covering his eyes, watching his career go into the toilet. The defense attorney was saying, over and over again like a mantra, "I can't believe this! I cannot believe this!"

"What? What can't you believe?" I asked her finally. "You asked me a question. If I don't answer, I'm in contempt. If I do answer, you want me held in contempt. Lady, what answer are you looking for?"

"We can't direct you, officer," the judge said.

"That's right, because my answers are supposed to be true," I answered. "Based on the knowledge, which includes physical evidence and the guy sitting in court today."

There was a lot of hand slapping and gavel pounding until the judge directed the jury to disregard my answer, but it remained on record.

The next thing Vance did was fucking beautiful. Seizing the moment, which was totally chaotic, he said, "Your honor, I'd like to submit this wallet, paystub, social security card, and photo ID into evidence."

The judge allowed it.

Amazingly, the defense attorney, confused or just an idiot, didn't object! The items were submitted, and Vance presented them to the jury, one by one, for review.

I watched the jury as they studied the small plastic cards, then turned toward Miguel. The photo ID went through the front row, then the back row, each person nodding his and her head as they ID'ed the defendant for themselves. All based on the photo. It was a beautiful tactic. Just fucking beautiful.

The other thing the defense attorney brought up was money.

"Officer, I see that you acquired twenty-three hours of overtime over this arrest," she said. "Is that the reason you locked up my client?"

"No," I answered. "I locked him up because he committed a crime. Any overtime I acquired was the result of police action taken in response to a crime being committed. A chain of events. The overtime came last. It's not something we have control over. Also, I was in the hospital as a result of this, and as we all know, New York City emergency rooms don't move with lightning speed."

The jury chuckled. They seemed to like me. I was polite, cordial, and professional. The jury also liked Vance, you could tell. He's like a big teddy bear. Sure, during the course of the questioning I was occasionally a little hostile towards the lawyer, but in addition to me, Vance, and the judge, I don't think the jury liked her all that much either, and it showed. She was tense and combative. She took every objection and decision by the judge that went against her case personally.

Of the four guys on trial, one was cut loose because he wasn't an active player; the other one, seeing the way things were going, took "two to four" on a plea bargain. We were finally down to Pena and Vargas. Pena was going the full boat (all the way), because he had other cases pending against him in Queens. If he copped a plea, it could be used against him there.

The jury was out less than six hours before finding both Pena and Vargas guilty. Usually cops don't show up for the sentencings, but I did. I felt I had a real investment in this case. I'd spent hours and hours of my time driving Vance around Brooklyn. Plus, Vance and I had become good friends, and if he could win this trial—this stupid fucking trial that nobody wanted—it would give his career a real boost.

Then, all this other stuff came up. While Pena was in jail awaiting trial, he stabbed another inmate. So he had to answer for that. Plus, there were extradition warrants out for his arrest in Puerto Rico, which meant that when our system got done with him, he'd be extradited back to Puerto Rico for another day in court.

I remember waiting out in the hall when Vance came through the door. Just looking at the grin on his face, I could tell it went well. Vance took both my hands in his and shook them hard. Pena got a pair of eight-to-fifteen year sentences, running concurrently. But since there were two, he'd probably do the full fifteen before the Puerto Rican authorities got their shot at him.

9

EVEN IF you go into a case with the best of intentions, things can get horribly screwed up.

A good example of this was a rape/sodomy case I had when I was on the job about a year and a half—working midnights to eight. My partner and I were called back to the station house. The sergeant handed us a complaint report and pointed toward two women, a mother and daughter, standing just outside the gate in the precinct's lobby.

I read the report, which in short stated that the daughter came into East New York to buy crack. She bought her crack and ended up smoking it with the guys she'd bought it from. Somewhere along the way the whole scene turned bad—maybe she wanted more crack; maybe the guys went nuts from the high—something went wrong, because the guys told her she couldn't leave. They kept her in this house for three or four hours, raping and sodomizing her repeatedly. When they finally let her go, she called her mother and they both ended up at the precinct.

The daughter was this white girl, a typical "Jane Average" from Queens. At one point she had probably been pretty, but the drugs were already taking their toll. She had a hard look about her. The mother was short and a little overweight, maybe forty or forty-five, and it looked

91

like her daughter's drug use was taking its toll on her too. She looked tired, and not just because she had to wake up at four in the morning and drive into the ghetto to take her daughter to the precinct. They were working-class people, the father, if he was around, probably had calluses on his hands and worked hard for his money.

My partner and I took them to a quiet corner in the roll-call room, and the mother started right in about being pissed off and outraged. Her daughter's just been raped, I could more than understand it, but there was something in her tone that didn't sound genuine. Listening to her, I just knew that this was only the latest incident in a long line of shit the daughter's been involved in. The mother was acting the way she thought I expected her to act—angry and out for vengeance. But she was working too hard at it; you could tell she'd spent all the outrage she had a long time ago.

We put the mother and daughter in the back of the RMP, and the daughter directed us to a house on Montauk Avenue, just off Linden Boulevard. It was a duplex row house with boarded up windows and a steel reinforced front door with a white iron gate enclosing an upper patio in the front. It was long suspected as a drug location, one of many in the area, because of its easy access. You could make your drug deal, do a U-turn, and you're on your way back home to Queens or Long Island.

My partner requested backup and three or four cars showed up. We got one of the cars to escort the girl and mother to the hospital.

In every suspected rape case, doctors do what's called a Vitulo Kit or Rape Evidence Kit. It actually is a kit. It consists of a cardboard box, the lid stamped with a form that hospital, police, and forensic personnel fill out. Inside, there's a booklet outlining step-by-step instructions for collecting evidence.

It starts with "Step 1: Sexual Assault Questionnaire" and proceeds through "Fingernail Scrapings," "Pubic Hair Combings," vaginal, oral, and anal swabs. Fourteen or fifteen steps in all. All the swabs, slides, combs, and vials are in envelopes. Each envelope is stamped with a short questionnaire and detailed instructions on how to perform the test. When the doctor has filled all the envelopes, the kit's then sent down to the police serology lab, the results analyzed, and the box re-sealed as evidence.

The kit's designed to keep all the evidence intact and usable for court.

I watched the daughter leave for the hospital as I went up the stairs to the front-gated patio and rang the doorbell. No answer.

There were a couple of steps below and just off to the side leading to a basement apartment. We knocked on that door. No answer, but it wasn't reinforced like the front door.

One of the cops put his shoulder to it, and the door flew open. Everyone drew their guns, my partner doing a rapid head poke in the door before we slowly walked inside.

The place smelled of urine, decay, and natural gas. And there was this weird lighting. A bare red bulb dangling from the ceiling provided the only light. The place was divided up by wooden partitions, like neck-high horse stalls.

I double-peeked into one of the stalls, holding a gun ready while my partner lit up the cubicle with his flashlight. Nothing.

A couple of the other cops were doing the same, moving quietly through the room. Nothing.

Then, just off the main room to the left, we heard rustling noises. We made our way back, and lying on the floor on a bare mattress is this guy.

"Police! Don't move!"

The guy rolled over, studied us sleepily and started to get up. My partner grabbed him, put the cuffs on, and one of the other cops led him out. Well we got one guy, anyway.

We kept moving through the basement. A small hall-way opened into a partially finished apartment with a decaying kitchen. No furniture and no signs of anyone living there. The place wasn't a crack house, not like any that I'd ever seen, anyway.

When we were sure nobody else was in the basement, we searched for the girl's personal property. Nothing.

At the far end of the basement, near some steps that lead to the backyard, there was another door. We kicked it in and went up a set of stairs to an upper apartment. At the top was another locked door.

I knocked on the door, "Police, open the door!"

Immediately a guy on the other side said, "No."

"Police . . . open . . . the . . . door!"

"No," he said again, very calmly.

"If you don't fucking open the door, we'll break it down."

"You need a warrant."

The guy had a point there. "Fine," I answered. "Have it your way."

So we put a cop on the front door of the house and one on the back door. I went back outside and rang the doorbell again. By now a couple of hours have passed, the sun's coming up, and the girl's back from the hospital. She sat in an RMP calmly watching me ring the doorbell.

Finally, the guy came out onto the patio with his girl-friend, but wouldn't open the gate. I went back to the car and asked the girl, "Is that the guy?"

She squinted and studied him carefully, then said, "Yeah, that's one of them. He's one of the guys who made me have oral sex with them then stuck it in my anus."

The way she said it sounded weird, technical and cold. Almost passive. Not embarrassed or degraded, not even pissed off. You see people more pissed off in small claims court. Maybe she was in shock, but it didn't sound that way.

I walked back up to the guy standing behind the steel gate. "Look, you got no place to go," I told him. "We got cops in the basement, cops in the back, and cops out front here. Where the fuck are you gonna go?"

He thought about it for a second, opened the gate, stepped out, and said, "What am I being arrested for?"

"Nobody said you're being arrested. You got a guilty conscience or something?"

"No, but that girl down in the car, she said I did something?"

"Well, now that you mention it, that girl says you committed sexual acts on her against her will."

He started to deny it, then the girlfriend jumped in, yelling and screaming.

Fuck it, I thought to myself, then spun the guy around and tried to cuff him while my partner tried to pull the girlfriend off of us. Finally, we got the guy cuffed, put everyone into RMPs, and drove back to the station house.

It wasn't until we came in through the back door at the precinct that I remembered it was Medal Day. The first fucking Medal Day the 7-5 has seen in years. The room was filled with cops in dress blues with their families. Little kids were running around. Wives were taking pictures and videos. All these cops brought their families in from Long Island, dressed the kids up nice for daddy's big day, and here we come walking in with two yelling and cursing rape suspects and a shy victim and her mother.

The noise level in the room dropped in half, and I could feel every fucking eye in the room on us.

"What is it? What's he got?" I heard whispered in these tight groups.

"Some rape/sodomy over on Montauk—crack-heads," someone whispered back.

One of the suspects, eyeing the scene, turned his head towards me, "What's going on, you havin' a party?"

"Shut the fuck up, asshole," I told him, pushing him forward towards the desk. I already know what's going to happen later. I'm going to catch a ton of shit for this in the locker-room. It's gonna go on for weeks.

As we led the suspects up to the desk sergeant, I could see in their expressions that nobody was happy about this. Every face in the room was silently saying, "Poss, you couldn't fucking wait. Christ, we got our fucking families here and you drag in these crack head butt-fucking pieces of shit. What a prick."

The girl ID'ed the guy who owned the house and the one we pulled out of the basement. The others must've split. Escaped forever unless one of the suspects ratted them out, which was unlikely.

The CO, done up in a crisp white shirt and dress blues, came over and I filled him in on what I had. It was a legit case, or so I thought. The complainant was present and had been checked out by the hospital. I had my evidence, a positive ID on the scene, and two perps. All the essentials. Because this was a felony sex crimes case, an ADA has to come to the precinct and talk to the complainant and the perp—if he wants to say anything. It's what's known as a "Riding Case."

Since it was a rape/sodomy case, I requested a woman ADA to talk to the girl and her mother. I decided to sit in on the interview and listen to the story again. The ADA was making notes and nodding her head every once in awhile. By the time the girl was halfway through her story, I could tell the ADA wasn't happy about it. She'd already sized up the case as shakey.

When the girl finished her story, the ADA said, "It's going to be a tough one."

The girl and mother looked up, questioning.

"For one thing, you were voluntarily in the house smoking crack," the ADA said. "You were there with the intention of committing an illegal act, then an illegal act was committed against you. Had you not been there, none of this would have happened. Do you understand?"

Now, I'm starting to get a little pissed off. Right off, the ADA started knocking the case down. Okay, the girl was there smoking crack. She admitted it. Maybe she made an arrangement with these guys to perform oral sex for drugs—a common trade-off in crackhouses—and the guys went too far. But deal with that *after* you deal with the rape. The last thing you want to do is intimidate a cooperative complainant/witness before she has to go in front of a grand jury.

A few hours later, we got the Rape Evidence Kit back from the hospital and had it sent to the police lab for serology tests.

When the report eventually came back, it showed there were traces of semen in the girl's mouth, anus, and vagina. Good evidence there. I'm thinking that maybe this will get the next ADA who handles the case more interested than the first.

The 180-80 day came, and I went to court. The girl and her mother were no-shows. Now we only had half a complaint. I testified before the grand jury based on her testimony in the police report, the ID at the scene, the evidence kit, and its results. Based on this, we got an indictment.

A few weeks later, another court date came up, some preliminary thing, and the girl missed that too. I called up the mother, and she promised to bring her daughter down.

The next court date we had, she missed. And the next, and the one after that.

After each court date I called the mother, and she kept promising. Each promise less sincere than the last. No doubt, the daughter had already moved on to new horrors to inflict on this tired woman. I saw the whole thing heading to a dead end.

And the whole time, the ADA was looking at me like it's my fault. Finally, the case just vanished into the system, buried. Never to be heard from again.

*   *   *

I finished the training at the county academy in Barnstable, Massachusetts on Cape Cod and showed up at P-town's only police station and headquarters. At that time it was housed in the basement under town hall, but was soon relocated to a newly renovated and upgraded facility away from the center of town. The new building, once a funeral home, was a "shingled-cape" with a lot of windows, had a manicured lawn, and a secured lot in the rear. It had everything except valet parking.

They issued me a uniform, gun, equipment, and the option to work steady midnights.

I was a cop.

First thing, nobody wanted the midnight tour. I jumped on it. I knew from riding with the cops in Providence, Warwick, and Cranston that midnights were when everything happens. If I was going to see if I liked being a cop, I wanted to see the worst. I wanted to see the most action.

Suddenly I was on the street. In P-town they ride one man to a patrol car. So, there I was, 22 years old with a gun, a uniform, a nightstick, a car, and a radio. I'm the law. Holy shit.

During the summer months, P-town is eighty percent gay. Not only am I the law, but I'm a straight man in a gay community. In high school and college, you call your friends "faggots," "homos," even "cocksuckers." It doesn't mean anything. It's just stupid name calling. You might as well be saying, "Ya mother wears army boots." But all at once, I'm surrounded by "homos," "faggots," and "cocksuckers."

Okay, I said to myself, you wanted to learn, learn about these people. I had to learn where they were coming from and to overcome my own ignorance and homophobia. And I had to do it as a professional. This was the community I was sworn to protect and serve. This was the community I had to interact with as a cop.

Up until then, I didn't think I even knew a gay person. But I was wrong. One night, after I'd been working there a few weeks, I parked the patrol car and decided to walk the downtown. Something you could never do in East New York. It was a nice summer night with a cool breeze coming off the ocean. I got about two or three blocks down Main Street, and I saw this guy looking into a clothing store window. Nothing special about the guy, dark pants, dark shirt, and a sweater draped over his shoulders, the arms tied in front. But his face was familiar. Even from half a block off, he looked familiar.

I walked up casually to the guy to get a better look. Now I can see he's in his mid-forties, graying hair, and he still looked familiar. Then it hit me, the guy was Father Deering, one of the Dominican priests who taught at Providence College. I had him for ethics class.

When I got a few feet away, I said, "Father Deering?"

He kind of squinted, then answered, "Joseph, Joseph Poss?"

Well, he recognized me in uniform a lot quicker than I recognized him out of his.

I was about to say something else, when this guy walks up. He was about my age, maybe a little older, dressed casually in a sport shirt and slacks, and draped his arm around Father Deering's shoulder.

The priest looked a little embarrassed and shrugged it off. "Well, it was good seeing you again, Joseph," he said, then turned to leave only to be obstructed by his companion who said, "Who's this?"

"One of my students from the college," Father Deering said, still trying to make an exit.

"Nice to meet you," the guy said.

Suddenly the situation turned uncomfortably quiet, the guy still waiting for Father Deering to formally introduce us. Again Father Deering tried to get away with a "nice-to-see-you-but-I-have-a-plane-to-catch" good-bye. He tugged at his friend, nearly pulling him, before his companion managed a quick, "bye," toned with annoyance toward Father Deering's apparent rudeness. I didn't even speak, instead I just waved them off, turned, and scratched my head. "Yeah, really," was all I managed to finally say.

I watched as they turned and started off down the street. Two or three doors away, the young guy tried to hold Father Deering's hand, but he pulled back, then looked over his shoulder to see if I was paying attention.

"What's wrong?" the young guy asked, half-turning to Father Deering.

I never heard the reply, they were too far away by that time.

WHAT DO you want?

Tell me exactly what you want. Be specific. Be precise. Choose your words carefully. What . . . do . . . *you* . . . want?

What is the quality of law that you desire? What level of justice do you demand? What are you willing to pay for it?

Thirty times a day, a cop hears nothing but problems.

"My car was stolen."

"My house was robbed."

"I was mugged."

"My husband beat me."

"Dear God, they've killed my son."

Always hanging in the air in living rooms, on street corners, and in precinct houses, that question. "What are you going to do?" Sometimes it's asked out loud; a lot of times it's silent and assumed—but it's always there. So is the demand, "Do something!" But cops know, they know it from the first week on the job, whatever you do, it's never enough. What they learn, eventually, is that there's not enough cops, juries, lawyers, judges, prisons, or justice in the world to fit all the crimes. What solutions are there? What are the answers the public wants to hear? What's their idea of justice? Isn't it something they've seen in the movies or on TV? Isn't it always fitting and appropriate?

But what, realistically, can a 22-year-old rookie tell a grieving mother? What words of wisdom has he amassed in twenty-two years of walking around on this planet that will ease by the smallest degree the pain of seeing her son rag-doll limp on a street corner, a halo of blood seeping out from a bullet hole in his head? What solace can he, a total stranger, a go-between, offer? Where in the Patrol Guide are *those* words printed?

This is what society is putting on the shoulders of twenty year olds newly dressed in blue. And when they come up blank or stunned or void of emotion, they hear, "You fucking cops just don't care."

I have seen 25-year-old cops turned cold and numb, transformed into blue zombies under the weight of it. They have passed the point of what they see or what they involve themselves in. They have reached the point where nothing penetrates. They zone out for eight and a half hours every day—every answer and every question out of their mouths is a Patrol Guide reflex. The sheer hugeness of it has turned them into cyphers, even to other cops. Lord knows what goes through their minds. It takes them three and a half minutes to change from civilian clothes into their uniform, then eight and a half hours of waiting before they can change back.

Just tell me what the fuck you want? What are you demanding from 22-year-old police officers? And how much would you demand from your son, your daughter, or yourself?

You can kill a child in New York and get off easy. The average sentence for child homicide in 1991 was 1.3 years. If it's your kid, there's a good chance you'll get three or five years of probation. But don't steal—don't you fucking steal money—because the average sentence for armed robbery was a minimum of four years. Sell two or more ounces of coke, mandatory 15 years.

Of all the jobs you can catch, working with the Bureau of Child Welfare (BCW) is probably the worst, next to runaways. BCW personnel need and demand police escorts when they remove children from a home. Oddly, pathetically, our agencies aren't allies in the war against child abuse. Cops understand that BCW is under-staffed, underpaid, and not very prompt in coordinating efforts. What city agency is fully staffed, well-paid, and efficient?

But a lot of the time, BCW short-cuts their work by calling precinct desk sergeants and giving a complaint number, a brief synopsis of the case, and requesting that a sector unit go to the address to see if the children are there and pull the kids out—all without an agency work-er being present. But they will meet you at the precinct later.

The problem is, and most cops are slick to this, BCW never shows. And there you are, babysitting a welfare case at Brookdale or Kings County Hospital pediatrics. Then you babysit some more at the station house until you—not the sergeant or BCW—make all the notifica-tions, do all the paperwork, and then drive the child to a foster care facility: either a private home, where a sleepy-eyed foster parent prepares a make-shift bed on a couch, or an institution, where they sleep in a dorm room.

This is why a lot of cops request a complaint numb-er, a BCW case number, a BCW case worker by name, and an estimated time of arrival at the precinct. Then the waiting game begins. If BCW is a no-show, the cop makes another notification. If no BCW personnel are available, then suddenly, neither are the cops. And another kid falls through the cracks in the system.

When it works like it's supposed to, BCW and the cops go to the house together at two, three, or four in the morning. The entire family is disturbed, the chil-dren awakened and removed from their beds, and taken to a local hospital for evaluation before entering the system.

If they're fortunate, they land in a foster home where there is enough caring, food, and clothing. If they're lucky, they are adopted. But a lot of times that BCW visit is an entrance into a system the kids will never escape. They might travel from foster home to foster home, then to Spofford Juvenile Correctional Facility, and on to state prison. From Dr. Dentons to death, they live their lives in state-run facilities.

We showed up at one house, the only house in a row of deteriorating buildings with actual glass windows, not sheets of plastic or planks of wood. It may not seem like much, but that glass was a good omen. Then we saw that the front door was broken off its hinges, bullet holes, old and new, scattered across it. That was a bad omen; it spelled out drug location as plainly as if they'd hung a sign.

Inside smelled of decay and urine. The wooden stairway tilted, like a fun-house feature, from the sinking foundation. The paint was peeling off the graffitied walls, and the hallway was lined with kids' toys, busted trikes, and baby-doll carriages—stuff that even crackheads wouldn't steal.

The apartment was on the second floor. My partner and I left the BCW team, a man and a woman, in the hallway, while we headed up the stairs. When we knocked, a woman answered, her voice muffled and scared through the wooden door.

We identified ourselves and the door opened, slowly, tentatively, the security chain still in place. Suddenly, the door was slammed shut by the husband.

"Police! Open the door!"

We heard them inside arguing. The wife kept trying to open the door, and he kept shutting it.

This routine was repeated three or four times until, finally, she got the door ajar more than two inches and

I jammed my nightstick through the opening. My partner took a quick step back and kicked it in. The force knocked the husband to the floor.

As we crashed through, the guy came out of a crouch and ran for the bedroom.

"He's got a shotgun in there!" the wife screamed. "He's got a gun!"

I took off after the guy and caught him at the bedroom doorway, throwing myself at his knees and tackling him back to the floor.

As I'm wrestling with this guy in his underwear, a little girl, five or six, appeared at another doorway, just in time to see me subduing her father. Suddenly she started to cry as I was trying to cuff him. Then the wife started crying.

When I finally got the guy cuffed and to his feet, I asked him his name.

"Find out if this is the guy," I said to my partner.

Stepping back out into the hall, he shouted down to the BCW people, who refused to come up the stairs. They'd been joined by two techs from EMS who wouldn't come up the stairs either. Nobody's coming into the apartment, except the cops.

The place was a mess. I can remember looking through the doorway to the kitchen and seeing the pots and pans, encrusted with food, piled high in the sink. It's strange what you remember, because I distinctly remember a lightbulb, just a bare bulb hanging from the kitchen ceiling, and how the living room floor was littered with dirty clothes—kids' and adults' clothes—and the bright plastic colors of broken toys scattered all around.

It was winter, and the heat was turned all the way up. It must have been eighty degrees in there, and I was sweating from the heat and from struggling with the guy.

Over all the crying, I heard my partner talking to the BCW team, but I couldn't hear any of their answers. He shouted something else, and fifteen seconds later he came back in saying, "Yeah, it's confirmed. This is the guy."

"Fuck you!" the guy shouted as I pushed him back to the floor. "This is my house. This is my family! I have a right! That's my right, so fuck you!"

"Yeah, fuck you too!" I shouted, pushing his face forward, then bent down to pull the guy up to his knees. I turned him to the wall as my partner picked up the little girl and started talking to her softly, trying to get her to stop crying.

"This is my fucking house, you understand that?" the guy screamed. "You have no right. No fucking right!"

"You have the right to give your daughter syphilis?" I asked the guy, talking right in his ear and yanking hard at the cuffs in an upward jolt. "You have the right to fuck your own daughter?"

"Fuck you!"

Somehow I managed to get the guy dressed in pants and shoes.

On a court order by BCW, the little girl went in for a checkup a few weeks earlier and tested positive for syphilis. So did the father. Two plus two equals four. As soon as they were able, BCW moved on the guy.

"Don't you fucking resist me, you scumbag," I told him as I moved past my partner, the little girl, and the mother out into the hall. "Don't you fucking resist!"

"This is my house!"

"Well, now you're going to leave it," I said. Then to my partner, "Wait 'til I get this asshole down."

I pulled the guy out into the hall. In the dim light I could see the BCW people and EMS, waiting at the bottom of the stairs, their faces turned up towards us.

The guy was still mouthing off belligerently. "It's okay, it's okay, you lock me up. And when I get out, I fuck her again. Huh, what you think about that?"

No shame, no repentance, no guilt.

The guy kept talking, his lips moving, but I couldn't hear him. He was like a television with the sound off. I froze, not out of fear, but because of something else. It was as if a huge wave of disgust washed right through me. I forgot about the uniform I was wearing—the thick blue skin that was supposed to conceal my emotions faded away. Nothing but contempt and anger for this parasitic fuck was left.

I turned back toward him, mechanically, my eyes blank, looking right through him. I chested him back, up against the wall, propping him up with my left forearm across his chest. I brought my right hand down and punched up with a closed fist. One, two, three shots to the balls.

He gasped in a sharp breath of air, his face blanching before his knees gave out. Still at the top of the stairs, then he moved not much, but a little, trying to squirm away. I picked him up by the belt and collar and heaved him forward, watching him tumble down the rickety stairs.

Everyone at the bottom took a giant step back as the guy landed at their feet, with me running down behind him. As soon as I hit the ground floor, I picked him up, put him against the wall, and kneed him in the balls one last time.

Behind me, the BCW lady gasped.

"This is what you wanted, isn't it?" I asked, turning toward her. "Isn't this what you fucking wanted done?"

Suddenly it got quiet in the hall, just the guy's ragged breathing and the little girl's crying upstairs. The BCW team and EMS were staring, wide-eyed, jaws unhinged.

"That's what you wanted, isn't it?" I asked again. "You heard what he said. You fucking well saw him resist! And that's what you wanted done."

Nobody, including EMS, BCW, the wife, or the husband, ever signed or filed a complaint against me. As expected, the kids were placed into foster care, and the mother was found negligent. The father went to prison, where I hope he spends the rest of his life. The jail-house code of justice is not kind to child molesters. "Short-eyes," as they're called, are bound and gagged and sexually tortured by other inmates.

But I was right. I was dead on right. That is what they wanted. They wanted to see that guy in a little pain, but no more than their consciences would allow. For once, they wanted to see some measure of justice for themselves. Not by their own hands, but by some-one willing to cross over from the civility to barbarity, then back again.

That's what they wanted done as they looked at that little girl crying because we, the police, were taking her and her father away. She was crying because she knew instinctively that things would never be the same again. Whatever pain she had suffered in the past, her life was now taking a new, uncertain and frightening course.

We knew this because we had seen it before in oth-er homes in the middle of the night. And all of us— my partner, the BCW team, and EMS—knew that there were no other choices because of what the father had done.

Everyone in that paint-flaked, bullet-prone, sagging hallway in the middle of the night had heard the details before. We had read BCW and police complaint reports or heard the testimony in court. We had seen the chil-dren. The victims were not material for news stories or textbooks. They were fragile and fearful beings.

He had taken that little girl, his own daughter, removed her clothes, fondled her genitals, forced her to perform oral sex on him, and probably forced himself inside of her. More than likely there was blood and tissue damage. The encounter would have left her emotionally scarred as well.

Those are just the details. Repellent, uncomfortable, and unpretty as they are, you have not seen the faces, heard the crying, or cursing, or felt alone and helpless in the face of a child's fear.

Tell me now, what is the justice you require?

Would your conscience have allowed you not to punish him?

He had made her a victim, betraying a trust so basic that even animals do not violate it. And, as a result, he had sent his daughter into a system incapable of love, warmth, or nurturing, but still better than what he had to offer.

He had forced an imperfect system and the people who serve it to rescue his child, only to subject her to something that may have been better, but was still less than what was right or decent or what she deserved.

She's out there somewhere. She didn't stop existing that night. It's been years since I've thought about her, but even now, I feel my chest tighten and eyes burn with the re-telling. She'll still be out there long after you read about and forget her. And for however long she lives, she'll have been robbed of something vital and essential.

Ask yourself what you feel, even though you've never seen twenty, thirty, or fifty of these animals slip through the system unscathed. Listen to your conscience. What measure of justice would you ask in that hallway on that particular night?

Isn't that what the public wants? Don't they want some sense of justice no matter how twisted? But they want it done quietly, under cover of night while they sleep. They want it done without offering consent or accepting responsibility.

They want it done the way the garbage is picked up from in front of their homes.

NEW YORK had the first ambulance service in the world. It was started in 1869 with horse and buggy teams out of Bellevue Hospital in Manhattan.

Today, you can ask any cop and he or she will tell you that New York City's EMS techs and paramedics are the best. These are some very heroic people.

They chase the radio all day and all night. By law, if you call 911 and request an ambulance, they're required to show up. That means they respond to 900,000 calls a year in New York; almost 2,500 calls a day. A lot of the time these calls are bullshit. Someone's sick and needs a trip to the hospital emergency room for a couple of aspirin, because they have a sprained ankle, or "just aren't feeling right." If it's two in the morning, freezing cold out, and you don't have a car, EMS is a door-to-door limo service. As a tech once told me, "You might as well put a taxi medallion on the hood and a meter on the dash." Each of these trips costs five hundred bucks. A hundred for the ambulance trip and four bills for the emergency room visit. Since a lot of people don't have insurance, the hospital rarely gets paid.

If you live in a place like Shaker Heights and you or your kid is sick, you call your doctor—some Marcus Welby family friend internist type—hop in your Volvo, and meet him at the hospital or his office. You probably visit the doctor once or twice a year for minor illnesses and checkups. And when you do, someone fills out your full-coverage insurance forms, assuring payment.

If you live in the ghetto, you hit the ER for medical attention. No checkups in between visits. When you're sick enough to be worried, you go to the ER, register at the intake window, then wait in a room filled with molded-plastic chairs that looks more like a bus station waiting room than a hospital. Up on the wall, there's a television playing, and forty or fifty people staring blank-eyed at it. Children cry from pain, boredom, and hunger.

It could take two to three hours before the nurse, overworked and exhausted, takes your temperature, blood pressure, and pulse and asks you the usual mundane questions as part of the triage procedure.

Depending on how sick you are, it could take a few hours or eighteen to twenty-four hours before you get looked at by an attending intern who's functioning on four hours of sleep in the last three days. The interns probably figure that if you've waited that long and haven't dropped dead, you must be serious about being sick.

Triage is a tricky thing in East New York. On bad nights, I've seen hospital waiting rooms packed to standing room only; the trauma units are backed up out into the hall with gurneys holding gunshot victims, auto accident amputees, and domestic dispute knockouts as EMS crews keep stacking them in. Meanwhile adults with broken bones, old people in pain, and feverish children stare blankly into the TV at Jay Leno's monologue out in the waiting room.

In places like East New York, most EMS crews wear bulletproof vests under their uniforms. They see the worst of it. Absolutely. They're the M.A.S.H. units of the ghetto. Like cops, they'll go into drug locations, tenements, and housing projects. They'll run into places, without guns, that would make the hair on the back of a cop's neck stand on end, then focus their full attention on the trauma at hand.

Never stationary and always on call, EMS drives around all night—their ambulance, or "bus" as it's referred to by emergency personnel, is their patrol vehicle. They have their own sectors, their own jobs. If by chance they witness a crime in progress, they radio it in to their dispatcher who relays it to our dispatcher. Because they're not in blue and whites (RMPs) or blue uniforms, people in the neighborhood take for granted that EMS overlook the street environment because it's not their job. But EMS knows the street. When you share steady shifts, you get to know the techs and paramedics working. And they get to know you. They'll work with you. Like cops, they know what a perp looks and acts like. I've seen them, against all regulations, follow suspects in the "bus," hanging back and radioing in the "perps" description, direction of flight, and location of witnesses and complainants. If they see guns on the street, they'll tell you. There's a special bond between cops and EMS. We complement each other in our efforts.

But this is the great thing about EMS and cops. I've seen drug dealers shot and lying in a pool of blood on the street. The guy could be a stone killer, but he's been shot and is dying. Cops will kneel over the guy, take the gun out of his hand and go over the radio, "RUSH THE BUS! RUSH THE BUS! CENTRAL. I'VE GOT ONE GOING OUT OF THE PICTURE (dying fast)!" And when EMS gets there, they'll fucking break their balls to save the guy. In two seconds, they'll have his clothes cut away, mass-pants (pressure packs) on him, an oxygen tube snaked down his throat, and an I.V. plugged into a vein.

Everyone on the scene knows the guy's a scumbag drug dealer. They know that if he'd been just a little quicker on the trigger, then there'd be another guy laying out on the street, and he'd be the perp. Yet, they're running around trying to stabilize him, to bring him back "into the picture." I guess that's a real commitment to the work. You do your best, you don't want to fail. If that guy dies, in the eyes of the public, you've failed.

On the other hand, if he dies, cops, EMS, everyone will stand around saying, "Good, that piece of shit died. Fucking drug dealer." I've been in a couple of situations like that. The fuck died, and it always felt bad, not out of any sense of remorse, but because it makes you and EMS look bad to the public. And you're a little pissed off at the guy for dying too. The guy was a prick; he broke the law, disrespected cops and society, and the last thing he did was die, as if he did it on purpose, just to make us look bad in front of a crowd.

There's always a crowd. Out on the street, you're always working in front of an audience. And they always want to see more. More blood. More gauze. More tape. Backboards. Gurneys. Neck collars, air tubes, defibrillator and portable EKGs. They want to see all the techno-gadgets. They want the truck emptied down to the last Band-Aid. They want to see all the props that Roy DeSoto and Johnny Gage used on "Emergency."

EMS will get to a scene where some guy is "doing the fish," flopping around on the sidewalk foaming at the mouth with a bullet in his heart. And inevitably someone will ask, "You gonna zap him?" What he means is defibrillate him—give the heart an electrical shock to restore cardiovascular rhythm.

When the cops and EMS ignore him, he'll say, "You gotta zap him."

If that guy goes out of the picture, that asshole will stand around nodding like Doogie Howser, saying, "You should have zapped him. The man would be alive today if they had zapped him."

I remember arriving at the scene of a shooting on the corner of Sutter and Vermont Avenues. A fat guy—at least 320 or 350 pounds—who was a known dealer was splayed out on the corner. When my partner and I got to the scene, he was propped up on the sidewalk in front of his drug location. He had been shot ten times! I counted the holes, no exit wounds. He had three or four gunshots to the leg and thigh, three gut shots, a couple of shoulder shots, and a groin shot. All around cars were riddled with bullet holes. I estimated forty or fifty shots had been fired.

Witnesses said a van drove by, and two guys jumped out and just lit up the corner with automatics.

"Okay, man, who shot you?" I asked, starting to search him. "Who did this to you?"

"Don't know," the guy says, groaning, "Why you searching me? I'm the one that's shot."

My partner's searching the five or six of his crew still bold enough to stick around, putting them up on the wall. But by the time we arrived, too late, all the guns had been tossed.

"You don't know? Who shot you?"

"Man, I don't fucking know!"

Yeah, like a perfect stranger is going to come by and cap off fifty rounds just for grins. Obviously it was a rival drug gang, but this guy wasn't about to give them up to the cops. His buddies weren't talking either. And he's complaining, the whole time, he's complaining. "Why aren't you doing your job? What's the matter with you fucking cops?" This fucking guy, he's got ten bullets in him and he's nagging. Not moaning, not begging, but whining.

All his fucking buddies are agreeing, chiming in regularly like a Greek chorus.

My partner gets on the radio, trying to get an ETA for EMS. But I knew just from looking at the guy that he wasn't going to die. Because of all the fat, the wounds had seized up. You'd need something bigger than a "nine" to hit this guy's vital organs. There was blood, but not as much as you'd think. Most of it was coming from the groin wound.

A few seconds later, EMS pulled up, and they started cutting his clothes away. It's two in the morning, and this guy is stark naked on the street. He's like a huge beached whale, with the lights from our car and the "bus" lights shining on him.

By now, more sector cars are showing up. They want to see the show. The guy's totally illuminated. Lit up like a night game at Shea. All up and down the block, people are sticking their heads out the window to get a look. He's center stage.

"How's it look man?" he asked me, probably because he didn't want to disturb EMS, who were vigorously working on his wounds.

Crouching down by his head with my hands on my knees, I said, "Doesn't look good man, they shot your package." It wasn't much of an observation, what was left of his dick was just a bloody flap hanging down between his legs. The bullet had gone clean through it before lodging itself in his thigh.

"What? What's that man? They shot my piece off! Man, it feels warm down there!" he said, panicked.

"You know that ain't right," one of his buddies offered shaking his head, and the rest of the crew murmured in agreement.

I have no doubt they had seen it too, before I did, but none of them wanted to be the one to break the bad news to him.

"They shot my man's dick off," another of his friends said to the gathering crowd. "Phsst . . . just shot it off."

"Yo man, they shot your dick off," a third one confirmed.

By now there was a small group gathering, and you could hear the news spreading through the crowd in whispers. It was like people *enjoyed* saying it, "Yo, they shot his dick off." "Man, they shot his fucking piece." "Ah man, I can *feel that*." Again and again, people were repeating it. A couple of the male onlookers shifted nervously, their faces showing empathetic pain before their hands went down to their own genitals for reassurance.

When I looked over, I saw my partner at the edge of the crowd keeping people back. Glancing over his shoulder at me, he started laughing, then buried his chin to his chest. Cop humor. A second later, I felt my face break into a grin, and I started laughing.

One of the paramedics dropped a large gauze pad over the fat man's groin. Instantly, it was soaked with blood.

"What are you laughing at?" the fat man asked. "What's so fucking funny?"

"Man . . . they shot your dick off," I said, grinning at him. "You sure you don't know who did it?"

Now, here's this guy, a man feared in the community. A big-time drug dealer laying out on the street, his grotesquely fat body no longer hidden by clothes. Naked, completely humiliated, his manhood shredded by a nine millimeter round. If he stays in the community when he leaves the hospital, he'll forever be known as the guy who got his dick shot off. He'll check out of the hospital, get a gun, and kill the shooters. Then kill the guy who hired the shooters, and everyone vaguely related to them.

But for the rest of his life, he's going to walk down the street and some kid is going to whisper to a friend, "Yo, that's the fat man who got his dick shot off." Not a great way to inspire respect, much less fear.

Now the fat guy starts screaming for EMS to put him in the ambulance. They're still trying to work on him, but he wants to get to the hospital. Probably thinking about the wonders of microsurgery.

"When I get outta the hospital I'm gonna get that fucker," he started to scream. "I'm gonna kill that motherfucker."

"Forget about it man, your piece is history," my partner said.

"Yo, that's cold," one of his crew said, trying to hold back a laugh.

"Don't say it, don't say *that*," the fat man groaned.

When the paramedic stood up, everyone got quiet. The problem was, how to get this guy onto the backboard, onto the gurney, then lift him three feet off the ground to put him into the "bus."

The paramedic scanned the crowd searching for muscle, first at the cops, then at the drug dealer's crew. Nobody was coming forward. Finally, ordering a couple of his crew to help lift, they were able to wedge the board under him. Then two crew members and EMS strained and grunted, hoisting the backboard from the ground to the gurney.

All the while, the guy is still complaining, telling them to take it easy.

Once they had the guy on the gurney, the procedure is to lift the patient up and into the back of the "bus." The gurney's forward momentum forces its wheels to lock into a mechanism at the front of the cab. This keeps the gurney and patient stable during the ride to the hospital.

It was a real physics problem. They were holding 350 pounds of dead weight in place, which meant they would need more forward and upward thrust than normal to get him into the "bus."

Bouncing slightly as they dropped the gurney along the cab's floor, they finally managed to load him in.

He lived, as we knew he would, but must have entered a new line of work.

As with any other job, some EMS techs are good, and some are exceptional. The whole job is preserving life long enough to get to the hospital, after that a doctor takes responsibility. But on the scene, they have to look at the situation and respond. What should they do, ventilate or shoot the guy up with something to raise the heartbeat? Something to clot the blood? They have to make these decisions in an instant.

I know a lot of outstanding techs, but one paramedic, Tommy, is absolutely the best I've seen under pressure.

We had a radio run, a 10-53 with a 10-54, which is a car accident with injuries. Someone ran a red light at a high speed at the intersection of Linden Boulevard and Fountain Avenue; a multiple-lane intersection with access roads, side streets, and all kinds of roads feeding into an open center.

When we got there the place was a mess. There were all these cars, just crumpled like tin cans. It looked fucking hopeless: bodies, blood, pieces of chrome, taillights, glass—like some kind of war zone.

I headed toward the most badly damaged car I saw, leaned in through the shattered window on the driver's side, and checked to see if the guy was dead or not. If you'd have asked me right then, I'd have said the guy was gone. The seat was pinning his chest right up against the steering wheel. Both his legs were crushed, and the windshield was bubbled outward from an impact that left his face a bloody mess. You couldn't even make out his features.

He was slouched forward and tried to mumble something, but I interrupted, "It's going to be okay. We got EMS here. Just hang in there." You know, false optimism. The things cops say just before they know someone's going to die. If they don't die, then you're a hero. If they die, hey, so I was wrong.

Soon, there were cops everywhere, EMS "buses," FD (Fire Department) apparatus, and RMPs cordoning off the intersection. Flares were lit, a couple of other cops were directing traffic around the scene, while FD started to hose down the gas. Everyone was doing their jobs. It was like a fucking circus, all the lights strobing, radios crackling, and uniforms barking commands. All these uniforms running around from one wreck to the next, critiquing each victim's condition, and prioritizing their aid.

I decided to stick with one guy, talking to him to keep him conscious. Tommy suddenly jumps up on the smashed hood of the car, pulls away a couple strips of shattered glass, leans in through the windshield, lays over the dash, and begins to work on the guy.

I know and Tommy knows, as soon as they cut that guy out and take the steering wheel's pressure off his chest, he's dead. There was no way to stabilize his BP (blood pressure) and stop the internal bleeding.

Tommy hooked the guy up to oxygen anyway and delicately put a neckbrace on him. He called over a couple of techs to stand by with a backboard and masspants.

They shoo me away, and get a couple of firemen to cut the passenger door away. Then they tried to get the mass-pants on him while he was still in the car. No room. No go.

The only way to do it was to cut the steering wheel away, pull him out onto the backboard, rush him into the pants, and inflate them fast enough to sustain pressure. I watched as the firemen used the jaws of life to cut away the driver's door and then started working on the steering column. Hands were reaching in for this guy from every direction. Power saws were going and steel was cut. The whole time, Tommy was still over the hood and dash working on the guy, never losing his rhythm or concentration.

As soon as they cut the column away and the pressure was off, the guy gasped, his eyes rolled upward, then started fluttering. He went unconscious. One, two, three, they had him out of the car, on the board, into the inflated pants and stabilized at a decent pulse. All this took maybe 35 seconds. Two minutes later, they had him in the "bus" and on his way.

Unbelievably, the guy made it. He's got Tommy to thank. They'll never meet again, and he won't even remember it. He'll wake up in the hospital, disoriented, and drugged to the gills for the pain, never knowing EMS saved his life.

It's an odd thing to think about for any length of time. All these people who rush in with the experience, training, and judgment to extract life from the confusion and chaos that always accompanies tragedy. At a shooting or a car accident, EMS focuses on the heartbeat. When a building collapses or house burns, FD shows up and works until the last body is accounted for and the fire is out.

The ability to bring order to the hopelessly chaotic is the thing cops envy on some level. No one cop can do everything. Chaos persists, and tragedies continue, one after another, with no sign of abatement. But the cop will never admit defeat, enduring to persevere.

12

NEW YORK'S *Bravest* is what NYC calls its firemen. Who
started calling them that? Some smart public relations
guy who worked for the Fire Department. They gave
themselves that title. But *New York's Finest* is what
NYC calls its cops. The *people* of New York City gave
us that title.

A crackhouse burns and there'll be a couple hundred
vials, scales, and record books scattered across a charred
floor. But no money.

Rumors follow.

Where's the money?

What happened to the fucking money?

The rumors aren't even whispered. Shrugs are given
in reply. Nobody talks about it. Nobody even wants to
think about it.

"That crackhouse over on Williams burned."

"What'd they recover?"

"Two thousand vials, a couple of scales, paraphernalia."

"Any money?"

"FD was there."

The silence itself is code. The message, unspoken, is
simple. Firemen steal. They stuff the cash in their boots.
Firemen pinch enough to finance vacations, to take the
family to Florida with drug money. *"You've just put out*

121

a four-alarm on Williams Avenue? What are you going to do now?" "I'm going to Disney World!"

To speak of these things is more than unpleasant, it's dangerous. And nobody crosses that line, it's better to let the stories die as rumors, removed from the public.

This is what makes the papers in New York: A cop arrests a fireman for some infraction. A cop and a fireman duke it out over who handles some disaster. Who responds first? Who's in charge? Who is going to be the hero?

But it isn't about being a hero. It isn't the protocol of carnage that's in question. It's about money. It's about which department gets its budget increased. It's about union arbitration negotiations, setting standards for salary parity and pay increases. It's about media coverage and internal reports used as leverage at the bargaining table.

It's about politics. When the city doesn't meet its budget, it closes firehouses and threatens to lay off cops. Politics sets the brass, unions, and uniforms of both departments at each other's throats. They slug it out in the press, creating a rivalry with sound bites.

The truth is, anyone who needs help doesn't give a damn which uniform comes to their aid.

There was a building West of Penn, at 447 Riverdale Avenue, that everyone hated. A five-story brick apartment house fronted by a rusting fire escape and surrounded by other tenements, with a variety store on the corner.

The place was a known drug location. Five or six guys always hung around: steerers, runners, and hitters. All the street-level doors were heavily reinforced against cops and rivals. At the front of the building, an opening from the sidewalk led down three or four steps into a small tunnel lined with storage rooms. At the other end of the tunnel was a central concrete courtyard littered with trash. The dealers set up a small peephole through the steel door of one of the storage rooms.

All the dealing was done through the peephole. Money would go in through the hole and crack was passed back out. A human vending machine. The supply was brought down from an apartment on the top floor. The beauty of it was the dealers didn't have to leave the building. They could seal off the building's entrances with their crew or posse (armed guards), then move money and drugs through the halls and crawl spaces with a minimum of exposure. By the time any street cops or a special detail, like TNT (Tactical Narcotics Team), broke the door down, the suspects would be long gone.

On slow nights, we'd get a couple of cars, pull up on the place, and throw the steerers and lookouts up on the wall while one or two cops snuck down into the tunnel and waited by the door the dealers dealt through. After a couple of minutes, when they thought they were safe, we'd tap on the door to signal that a buyer was waiting. When the peephole slid open, we'd spray mace into it. Inside the dealers would be choking, cursing, and screaming. It was something to do on a slow night. Ghetto antics. Cops and robbers, East New York style.

Anyway, early one winter morning, about 1:30, we got a call for a 10-59, which is a fire with FD responding. I was partnered with this guy, Nicholas, a black cop who knew what "the job" was about and who knew the streets from growing up in Brooklyn. He was a good cop. He *was* Brooklyn.

We raced to the scene because both of us wanted to see this fucking building go up. We wanted to see fire put these scumbags out of business.

When we got there, the place was really lit. Smoke poured out windows and flames shot up from the roof.

There was a small crowd of people gathering outside across the street and pointing to the second floor. The building was occupied, and we couldn't wait for FD. Out of reflex, we raced inside. Halfway down the hall, we noticed the stairs covered in flames. The sight of it brought us up short.

It was eerie, like a river of fire swirling upward. The fire was fed by incoming air, sucked through the front door and out opened windows on the upper floors.

Both of us just froze watching it, mesmerized. Then I looked up and saw the fucking ceiling was on fire. Flames, like liquid defying gravity, eddied around over our heads. And down at the end of the hall, more flames.

We had to crouch because the heat and smoke were getting worse. It was the weirdest feeling, cold air was blasting in from the front door around my ankles, while my head felt hot, like it would ignite.

I looked at Nick and said, "What now, genius? We can run up those stairs, but there's no guarantee we're coming back down that way."

"Fire escape," he said. "Out front."

We headed back out front, pulled down the ladder, and climbed up. At the second floor, there was an old lady and a child, and they couldn't get their window open.

Nick turned and elbowed the window out, and the lady handed him a 3-year-old Spanish girl through the jagged opening. He took off his duty jacket, stuck the kid's legs through the sleeves, re-zipped it so she was in a sitting position, then lowered her down in this makeshift harness into some guy's upstretched arms.

I was still trying to get the old lady out. She managed to climb through the window. But frozen with fear, she wouldn't move off the fire escape. By then the fire trucks started to pull up, EMS following, setting up a joint effort. Meanwhile, people were coming down the fire escape, passing us, and dropping to the sidewalk on their own.

"Lady, we have to get out of here! Please!" I shouted at her. Frail and afraid, her hands were glued to the fire escape railing.

Two or three minutes later, I was still trying to move

this lady. A couple of firemen had somehow gotten above us and started breaking glass over our heads. They worked their way through the building knocking out windows, punching holes, and venting the roof to let the smoke out. They were trying to prevent the place from becoming superheated and exploding.

From where I was standing, it sounded like they were tearing the building apart. Glass was crashing down from the windows over our heads, shattering as it hit the fire escape above us.

A moment later, fire had almost completely engulfed the building and I couldn't lower the old lady down, even if she had let go, because flames were pouring out through the front door beneath us. Climbing down meant climbing into the flames. Heavy smoke was billowing out, so I couldn't breathe and my eyes were beginning to burn.

"Lady, we gotta get out of here!" I yelled. The only way down now was across a three-foot gap to the next fire escape platform. All I could think was, *Why is this so difficult?* We were only fifteen or twenty feet off the ground. It's as if we were stuck at the top of the World Trade Center.

Finally, this fireman came down the ladder. I climbed across to the next platform, and he picked the lady up, ripping her hands from the railing, and threw her at me. I managed to grab her and pull her across the space between the fire escape landings. She made her way down the ladder slowly, then a couple of cops grabbed her and lifted her off safely to the sidewalk. I followed her down.

As Nick and I walked back past the front door to the hallway, I looked inside. We'd been on the fire escape maybe ten minutes tops. It was completely engulfed in yellow and red flames. Fire covered every square inch. If Nick and I had gone in that way, we wouldn't have made it back out.

Nick and I wrote up the incident for departmental recognition and later received meritorious medals for our heroism and brave stupidity.

In the academy they showed us a training film of a fire. The whole film used just a single camera aimed at a mock living room—complete with television, sofa, chairs, drapery, pictures on the walls, carpets and lamps. The kind of living room that could exist anywhere, like in a furniture showroom, but you knew existed nowhere. It was too perfect. At the bottom of the screen was a digital readout to clock elapsed time.

First the curtains were ignited, just a small flame. The readout began spinning like an Olympic timer for the hundred meter dash. After thirty seconds, none of the recruits in the semi-lit classroom could take their eyes off it. Flames jumped from drapes to ceiling. Furniture ignited spontaneously from the heat. In less than two minutes, the whole room was covered in flames and smoke . . . *flashover*. In minutes nothing was left.

How do you fight something like that?

As a cop, you look at fires, really bad fires, and are overwhelmed. It's a force that, if left alone, will incinerate, melt, and turn to ash everything in its path.

You've seen its devastation—buildings gutted, cars charred down to base metal, windshields liquified. The morgue is filled with bodies burned beyond recognition. The fat turned to a slick sheen over the chest, legs, and arm muscles; the yellowed bones of fingers protruding from skinless hands.

You can't stop fire with words, a nightstick, or bullets. You can't arrest, process, or haul its sorry ass into court. It consumes everything, its progress governed by mysterious and immutable laws of nature.

Yet, in ninety-five-degree August humidity, these guys put on heavy canvas and rubber coats, boots, helmets and forty-pound oxygen tanks and run into burning buildings. In the middle of December, when it's four degrees outside, they're spraying water on buildings and each other—literally drenching themselves in it.

These fucking guys run into burning houses and collapsing buildings. They run into places that drug dealers have booby-trapped with sawed-through floors, nailboards, and rigged shotguns.

If you breathe in too much smoke, you can walk around for two or three days feeling fine, then just drop dead from a heart attack or smoke inhalation.

Being a volunteer fireman is not a job I'd want to do. But a lot of cops do it. A lot of city cops who live on Long Island are active volunteer firemen in their communities. So, not only do they have neighbors coming to them to fix parking tickets or quiet a neighbor's kid who's playing Guns 'N Roses at 11:00 P.M. but they're also constantly on call for fires.

You hear a lot about these other cops too. After two or three years on the job, they get sick of the bureaucratic bullshit, take the FD test and wait to "roll over" to the fire department. They want to leave PD because they see something better in FD. It's more than just the grass looking greener. It's the same pay, but without the hassles.

Firemen get four days off after a seventy-two hour jaunt.

They eat great meals because one of them is usually a gourmet chef.

They get to slide down that nifty polished brass pole we all wanted to slide down as kids. They publish cookbooks to benefit burn victims. And they pose for calendars in skimpy bathing suits.

Then there's the women. It's a fact: Women in New York love their firefighters. There's a romantic quality to it for them. Maybe it's something to do with fantasies of being carried effortlessly down a ladder and out of harm's way. It could be those pictures that portray a grim, sooty-faced fireman cradling a kid under his jacket as he races from a burning building.

Whatever it is, women in New York love firemen. You see them in Manhattan, all the firemen out at 8:30

in the morning, standing in front of the firehouse as the nine-to-fivers walk to the subway, womens' eyes shifting subtly to the line of firemen, their gait slowing just a trace as they pass. Young mothers sneak glances over rows of vegetables in the supermarkets, watching an engine company of firemen do their food shopping. Those women note with approval the careful comparison shopping and use of coupons.

The stereotypes are easy to make.

Cops eat donuts.

Firemen eat nutritious balanced meals.

Cops lift "Big One" cups of Dunkin' Donuts coffee.

Firemen lift weights between calls.

Maybe it's because they don't carry guns or aren't tainted by the violence of the street. Perhaps it has to do with all that downtime, where they get the opportunity to sleep, relax, and deflate. Cops aren't afforded that luxury. We're wound so tight for eight and a half hours straight, that there's never any time to exhale. It's relentless.

They're not a paramilitary organization. They show up at street festivals, parades, and block parties to let kids climb all over the trucks. They welcome the curious without suspicion and work fairly regular hours. And they don't have to shoot anyone either.

Cops may be noble, but firemen are brave sons of bitches.

The lines are clearly drawn. Fires out of control are bad. The firemen who put them out are good. With criminals, the only place that clear-cut line exists is in a cop's head.

When you're a cop, there are things you see that sear into your brain. They rearrange the chemistry in your skull so that you know you'll never forget them.

This is one that's forever tattooed across my gray matter. We showed up at a "59" (fire) at 1025 Hegeman. It was a nothing five-story apartment building, abandoned and used by crackheads.

We parked down the block next to a Chinese take-out place, away from the fire engines and the tangle of hoses and equipment jamming the street. A crowd of onlookers was gathered behind lines formed by the outstretched arms of cops, keeping them back. All of them watched the building, five stories of tan brick with smoke and flames coming out through the windows.

As my partner and I got out of the car, we saw a fireman at a top floor window. Behind him was nothing but flames. Then, unreal as it looked, I realized he was on fire. He was literally coming out through the flames, his arms waving as he tried to untangle himself from them.

The whole thing seemed to happen in slow motion. Who knows how long he'd been in that room, surrounded by fire and blinded by smoke: How long could it have taken him to find that window? I can't imagine the pain he must have endured, or how he was even able to summon the presence of mind to keep going. It must've taken an incredible force of will just to keep moving.

Emerging from the window, he stepped out onto the ledge, bracing himself in the frame. Flames lapped around his clothing as firemen below tried to raise the manned cherry picker toward him, the machinery working agonizingly slow.

As the basket came level with the window and began to swing toward the building, he jumped the ten feet from ledge to basket. The guy was like a fireball leaping across to the basket—moving through the air a hundred feet above the sidewalk—with pieces of his gear and clothing dropping off in flames.

He hit the basket hard, sending a shudder through the cherry picker as he slammed against it, catching its lip with arms that were on fire. The fireman in the basket grabbed him as a team below turned the hoses on them, dousing the flames.

A few seconds later, they had them on the ground and EMS was working on him, delicately wrapping him in gauze soaked with sterile water. They Medivaced him out, landing the chopper in the schoolyard down the street.

Through the 7-5 detective grapevine, we learned that the fire had been set by some crackhead bitch with an arson record. She probably used a buck's worth of gas and a disposable lighter to start the fire.

A week later, news came back to the precinct. The fireman had died, suffering first-degree burns over eighty percent of his body. The tragic irony of it all was, the very woman he went in to save had set the fire.

They called this one heavy (busy) firehouse, *The Pride of Sheffield Avenue*. It was the only building on the block, surrounded by a weed-filled, garbage-strewn lot littered with broken glass, abandoned cars, discarded tires, and old furniture. A strange sight in New York— one building adjoining a small parking lot with a razor-wire fence protecting firemen's private cars.

The guys at the firehouse decided to throw a party for a retiring fireman. Firemen and a couple of off-duty Transit cops attended. A bunch of them pitched in for beer and then drank it all. A couple of the guys walked half a block to the corner bodega, bought some more, then drank that.

When they showed up the third time, the bodega owner refused to sell them anymore beer. He didn't want his stock completely depleted for the night ahead.

Making matters worse, they wanted the beer on credit. The firemen left pissed. The bodega owner and a couple of neighborhood "crew" followed them out.

What happened next is only hearsay, but some kind of confrontation took place on the sidewalk in front of the store. Choice words were exchanged. A couple of party-going, off-duty Transit cops, watching from the firehouse, ran over. Either outnumbered or just flexing their "beer muscles," someone let a few "fuck you" rounds go into the air. Then they all ran back to the firehouse like a bunch of kids who just broke a neighbor's window.

The bodega owner was really scared. He called 911. There's only one problem: the bodega's a fucking drug location. So when the cops showed up, the bodega owner turned hesitant, hemming and hawing over his complaint. The dealers outside his door probably talked to him between the time he dialed 911 and when the first sector car showed up. Cops meant attention brought on their location.

It would have been chalked up to a 10-10 (shots fired). In East New York, "shots fired with no further information," is a nothing call. Every time a gun passes hands, the new owner goes up to a tenement or housing project roof and lets go with ten or twelve rounds to feel the recoil. On an average night there are hundreds of shots fired.

But a midnight lieutenant, known to overreact and exaggerate situations, showed up on the scene right behind the responding sector. The LT starts pumping the bodega owner for information, but the guy kept insisting it was just a misunderstanding, which it was.

Not satisfied, the LT went over to the firehouse and was totally stonewalled. No one knew anything. The LT was a known nutcase, but he wasn't a moron. He knew *something* had happened and wouldn't let it go. He was going to get to the bottom of it. Maybe he saw some kind of advancement or precinct promotion in it if he broke the "big bodega beer case."

He picked up the phone and started to make "notifications." Soon the DA's office got involved. What began as a misunderstanding now turned into a "riding case." The FD brass got involved. NYPD and Transit bosses got involved. The unions got involved. What a fucking abortion, as they say.

Days later, the LT's still bouncing around, asking everyone he can corner who'd worked that night about the incident. *Somebody must know something.* But nobody's talking. It was rumored that there may have been a couple of off-duty Transit cops involved, but they're still cops. And nobody was going to hand over someone else's job to this fucking headhunter.

What's more, somebody tipped off the press. The papers and local television news started running stories about it. Then not even the brass wanted to pursue it. Careers, big-money-twenty-year-careers, can be wrecked by a two-minute news story.

It's FD, let it die.

It's Transit, let it die.

It's bullshit, let it die.

We don't want it, let . . . it . . . die.

The brass, the unions, the cops on the street, the bodega owner . . . everyone is saying, "For Christ sake, just let it go."

But the LT saw himself as some kind of departmental savior and kept pushing the issue. He was going to get to the bottom of it. Soon, whatever tenuous relationships he had in the precinct itself, with Transit, and with FD evaporated. Nobody wanted to be associated with this penny-ante psycho-Serpico.

A month later he showed up at a fire and started directing fire equipment and rescue apparatus, bizarrely trying to override an FD battalion chief. He was out in the middle of the street for about ninety seconds when one of FD's hoses "accidentally" got away from the two fire fighters manning it. Doubtful this ever happened to these two guys before, because in the center of the confusion, with all that equipment and all those uniforms, the only person to catch the spray of water—and catch it in full—was the LT.

The force knocked him flat on his ass. Fifty cops and

firemen and a hundred bystanders broke out laughing as he lay there like a drowned rat.

What finally killed the big bodega beer case was that the bodega owner couldn't make a positive ID of any firemen or supposed "phantom" Transit cops. The DA's office declined the case, referring it to the FD's Inspector General's Office for "investigation."

The personnel that comprised *The Pride of Sheffield Avenue's* Engine Company 290 and Ladder Company 103 suffered a house rouse (transfers), scattering anybody who might have known anything to the four winds. An intelligent move by FD to CYA (cover your ass) in case of reprisal.

The 7-5 detectives closed the case's 61 (complaint report) as "menacing." A meaningless, dime-a-dozen complaint.

But what really killed the big bodega beer case was, they "let it die."

ALL OVER East New York, The Bronx, and Upper Manhattan are buildings owned by the city, seized for back taxes. Their windows and doors are sealed with tin or cinderblock. Fire Department markings indicate structural viability. You can drive down entire blocks and see nothing but spray-painted boxes with large Xs in their center, indicating extreme danger.

Slumlords who had collected rent for years walked away from them rather than invest in repairs. Those with more larceny and greed in their hearts torched them for insurance, then abandoned the property. They saw no future in East New York and no profits in repairs. These buildings, which were built with a pride long extinct, had been allowed to decay past a point of being habitable.

The shells of stripped cars litter Elton Street and Vandalia Avenue. Some are stolen, others abandoned. Vehicle chassis, engine blocks, and body parts, unusable and rusted from the elements, are left for the city's Sanitation Department to collect on flatbeds.

Newborns are abandoned in hospital nurseries, trash bins, and garbage chutes, their parents vanished.

This is a ghetto attitude. It's what the ghetto does to people. It teaches you to look at whatever's at hand, to use it until it's useless, then discard it without remorse. If it breaks, wears out, becomes shabby, or inconvenient

134

to maintain, you knew it would happen—knew it with the certainty of instinct. You're not entitled to surprise or regret.

One of the things you learn on this job, everyday, is that we live in a disposable world. People die and things break. The rules of the game may change constantly, but there is no getting around the inescapable drift towards decay.

As a cop, you find yourself closer to the mortality and wreckage than anyone else. You've seen so many bodies, randomly scattered throughout the precinct's sidewalks, streets, and storefronts, that death no longer has the power of shock or repulsion. You've seen the effects of neglect and time on people and things, in every form imaginable. Nothing lasts forever. Everyone dies.

You finish a soda. Throw away the can.

The girlfriend isn't winding your watch like she did a year ago? Dump her.

The wife found out about the new girlfriend? Divorce her.

You learn, day by day, that everything is disposable and everyone replaceable. The word is *fungible*. One can of soda is just as good as the next. Within reason, one piece of ass is just as good as another. One felony charge, just as appropriate as another. If the scumbag drug dealer doesn't do ten to fifteen for dealing, then he'll do five to ten for possession.

Save nothing but your own life. Whatever continuity people or possessions bring to your life is useless baggage destined for the junk-heap. The lesson you learn is not to let people too far into your life. Keep them at a comfortable distance. Draw the line where you feel comfortable, and put up a wall when you don't. But draw the line.

What are the choices? To tell other cops what you really think or feel? How can you confess a secret fear, weakness, or guilt? You risk the label of *coward* or *pussy*. Questions will be raised regarding your ability to deal with the street.

How are you going to bring a piece of the street back into your home without upsetting your wife? She'll sit up all night thinking that each time you leave for work you'll never come back. A common phobia. The truth.

Are you going to tell the Manhattan waitress you've been doing the Mattress Mambo with that you don't love her? She'll figure some devious way to let your wife know what's really going on.

What you do is tell other cops your war stories. You tell your wife you love her. And you tell the girlfriend as little as possible.

You keep everything together with silence, secrets, lies, and attitude for as long as possible. And hope when they fall apart, they all don't go at once. You drink your soda and throw away the can.

Cops learn this slowly. Over years of trial and error. It takes a long time before you realize that it's not just your attitude, but the entire department's attitude. Because the department is constantly telling you, "We love you guys! You're the best. The bravest. You're New York's Finest by God, and we take care of our own."

It's as if being a member of the department, especially assigned to an "A" or heavy house, such as the 7-5, makes you some kind of invincible hero. Sadly, after a while, you begin to believe this tripe. You want to believe it. Anything is better than the truth.

The truth is a bitter fucking pill. Let a cop just *appear* to make a mistake and the administrative brass will sell him out to the media, Internal Affairs, and the DA's office in a heartbeat. When public outcry demands that a cop be nailed to the wall, they give them one. For the brass, politicians, and the media, it's a casual sacrifice. And all too often, it only covers up the department's own errors in judgement. A lot of times the cop they hang is a scapegoat, smokescreening their own mistakes to silence the public and press.

You come to realize that you're one in more than 20,000 cops—not including brass, sergeants, lieutenants, captains, detectives, chiefs, or inspectors. You're infantry. You're expected to die. You're expendable. Maybe not you personally, but a percentage of street cops are expected to fall victim to car accidents, bullets, knives, and fire. The city pays insurance premiums based on how many cops die and are sued each year in the line of duty. Actuarial tables don't lie. They expect deaths, just as surely as they expect to put in orders for new RMPs, radios, and lost guns, yielding to the law of expendibility—you become an acceptable loss.

The moment you realize you are expendable is the moment that everyone and everything around you becomes expendable. Priorities shift to an agenda of personal survival. Everything about "the job" suddenly makes sense, and nothing is the same again.

This is how I began to see it—how I realized I'd adopted an expendable way of thinking.

There were two of them. At seven in the morning, a young Spanish woman and a Black woman were walking together from the subway to the factory where they worked. That's the way they usually got to work, finding safety in numbers. They'd board the trains somewhere in the Bronx, Queens, or other parts of Brooklyn and end up in East New York. Somewhere along the line they'd hook up, making the walk to the factory together in pairs or small groups.

They worked in a factory where they make shirts for Brooks Brothers, Lord Jeff, and a few other brands. The factory is one of a few pieces of light industry that remains in East New York. I can only imagine where those Wall Streeters think their button-down oxfords are actually being made. Maybe they have a quaint picture of happy craftsmen, painstakingly stitching their pinpoint oxfords together in a Saville Row-like tailor shop with Vivaldi playing in the background. Probably they don't think about it at all, though if they did, they wouldn't turn their thoughts to open floors the size of football fields, with minority women sweating, and the place filled with the sound of sewing machines.

This one morning, a couple of teenagers wearing gray hoodies, one of them carrying a gun, came up from behind the two women, snatched their purses, tore the chain off one's throat, and ran away. All the makings of a 10-32 (armed robbery).

I was working a perimeter, solo patrol, around a construction site of low-income housing projects when the call came over the radio. A brief synopsis: the perps' description, direction of flight, how many "minutes in the past," a complainant's location, and that a weapon was displayed. Rounding the corner near the location of the robbery, I spotted two males fitting the description.

I followed the suspects down a sidestreet. Keeping a safe distance, I radioed my location to central, saying that I had two "possibles fitting the description." Suddenly, they made (noticed) me and bolted.

I gunned the RMP up on the sidewalk and trapped one between the bumper and a fence. I jumped out, jacked (beat) his ass, cuffed him to the fence, and took off after the second perp.

By this time sector cars were coming from all directions. The second perp was half a block or more away when he turned and pointed a gun over his left shoulder at me. I dove between two parked cars. When I looked up over the roof of the car, I saw two RMPs cut him off. The cops had their revolvers drawn through their car windows, barking commands at the guy to drop his gun. Wisely, he surrendered.

By the time I'd retrieved perp #1, my RMP, and returned to the other cops, the recovered evidence was proudly displayed on the hood of an RMP—a loaded .25 caliber Raven automatic and ladies jewelry. Perp #2, wearing a gray hoodie, was handcuffed and bent face down, the booty and weapon inches from his nose.

In the rear of another RMP were two pissed-off complainants who made a positive ID. Beautiful.

Back at the Station House, the women were led into the roll-call room. The perps were put in the holding cell. I remember sitting across the table, looking at both of the women, and thinking to myself how beautiful the Spanish one looked—made even more attractive by the innocent look of fear in her face. Taking my cue from a couple of other cops to "hook up" and get her phone number, I went over and began talking to her.

I started chatting, then moved on from there. The other woman kept looking at me semi-suspiciously. As it turned out, the Spanish woman was recently separated from her second husband, had a young daughter, and was living with her cousin on Staten Island.

On one of my RDOs, I met her in Battery Park, at the top of Manhattan. She brought her cousin with her. All three of us walked around, small-talked, and then said good-bye.

Over the next couple of weeks, we met a few more times. By the third meeting, she felt safe enough to leave the cousin home. When we met at the park again, it began to rain. So we jumped in a cab and I took her back to my place.

I was living in the East Village at the time, on Avenue A, above the Pyramid Club, a trendy nightclub that was hot in the mid-eighties.

I remember, we talked about going out to a movie, then getting something to eat—typical New York date—but that was all talk, we never even looked up the movie listings. We were out of our wet clothes inside of twenty minutes, and doing the nasty on the couch. Then in the bedroom, 'tween the sheets. Then in the doorway, and finished up taking turns washing each others backs in the shower. Only to do it again under the spray of warm water.

Not only couldn't I believe how beautiful she was, but how I got over on her. I was fucking my robbery case witness. Somewhere in the four thick inches of printed pages that make up the Patrol Guide, there must be a section on how you shouldn't be screwing a witness on the sofa.

When I was 18 I was "requested to attend" the Cotillion Ball. My girlfriend invited me to her "coming out"— a formal presentation of a young woman to society. You rent a tux, assemble in the country club's grand hall, and are seated next to your date's mother. The young women, wearing elegant gowns, come down the stairs, where they are met by their fathers at the bottom. The whole event is very formal and serious. High society, Shaker Heights style.

A few months before, I'd lost my virginity to my girlfriend in her bedroom. It was a semi-planned event, an unspoken understanding between us that "this was going to be it." Her parents were at the airport picking up her sister. We figured we had two, maybe two and a half hours—a window of opportunity into which we had to cram sensitivity, romance, intimacy, and lovemaking. At least our own 18-year-old versions of them.

We did it with the same kind of polite formality as Cotillion. It was expected. We were co-conspirators, fearing discovery, her parents, and the possibility of failure. We did it once that first night and afterwards pledged love and the rest of it. We believed it would last, even as we scoured the room for any clues that might give us away.

I told my friends. She eventually told her friends. There were high-fives and giggles all around. Even then, we believed it would last. In my mind's eye there was a picture of us married with kids, a dog, a house, and a Volvo. A lifetime of passionate sex, as if her parents were permanently banished to the airport.

By the time I was sitting in that hall next to her mother, an extremely polite, petite, and socially proper woman, I was one of maybe a dozen or so guys there who'd bedded one of those young women walking down the stairs. All of us knowing they weren't so "pure," yet probably thinking it would last.

But in my apartment on Avenue A, sex was something else. It wasn't polite. It wasn't very innocent. I did it once, I wanted more. Twice, I needed more. This sex was like a drug. I took it greedily, knowing it wouldn't last, and never thinking about the consequences. There was a shameful kind of freedom in not caring about what she thought or felt. Whatever connection existed ended at whatever pleasure we could squeeze out of a few hours. It could have been anyone in that beautiful body she had. And the more we fucked, the more I felt like that.

It would end. I knew it would end. So it was better to make the most of it. Get as much as I could. In my mind, it was exactly what it was—great sex without a verbal commitment. If she wanted to believe it was something else—as I'm sure she did—I wasn't going to come clean. I knew it was going to end and when it did, there'd be no winner and no loser. But I convinced myself later that I'd won and she'd lost.

My father once told me, "Treat every woman in a relationship as if you were her first." It's the kind of advice that seems almost quaint now in an age when women carry their own preferred brands of condoms around like dental floss. It's good advice for Shaker, but irrelevant when you've reached a bottom line in your thinking of who is disposable and who is not.

The whole thing ended horribly. She took me to her apartment on Staten Island. A tiny place, her daughter asleep in the bedroom. I knew then, peering in through the bedroom doorway and looking at this little girl that wasn't mine, that it was time for it to end. I made up some lame excuse to leave, then never returned her calls. I moved to Brooklyn, changed my phone number, and left no forwarding information. She left messages and stopped by the precinct, her persistence finally wearing down until the calls and messages stopped altogether.

When I think of her now, I think of the sex, but also of my own greedy shallowness at that time. She was, in the end, expendable.

I drove all night from Dallas, Texas where I'd just finished taking their four-day exam and physical agility test. Now, I was on my way to NYC for their exam. At dawn I stopped at some "no-tell" motel with a pool in Jersey. I snuck in, took a shower and a swim, then headed into New York a couple of hours later, driving through the Holland Tunnel at rush hour.

The NYPD exam was being held at FDR High School in the Bronx at eight in the morning. When I pulled up, I couldn't believe what I saw. A line of applicants stretched from the entrance of the school, around the corner, then dispersed off into a "concert crowd" in the parking lot. Six or seven thousand men and women lined up for the exam. And I knew that wasn't the only testing location. All over the city, it was the same thing: thousands of people were lined up in high school gyms and classrooms to take the test.

They ushered us in on time and showed us to assigned classrooms. This high school was different than any other I'd ever seen before. Graffiti marked the walls, and the place had a feeling of disrepair and age about it.

We sat down at rickety fiberboard desks while uniformed proctors handed out the booklets. Instructions were given and the time limit announced. One hundred and four questions . . . six hours to complete. Sounds easy? It isn't.

I felt as if I were taking the SATs again.

We were fingerprinted for identification and security checks. The proctor spelled out detailed instructions, explaining the format in the simplest possible terms. The proctor spoke in monosyllables, like a first-time substitute English instructor teaching non-English-speaking immigrants.

Finally we opened our books and began.

Most of the test dealt with identification, memory, comprehension, and judgement. The questions started off easy, then became harder and harder, longer and longer.

Halfway through the test, a guy sitting next to me, maybe 19 or 20 years old, raised his hand.

"There's no talking during the test," the proctor said.

"I don't know what this word is, this 'played,'" the guy said.

The proctor sighed his annoyance, came over, leaned down over the book, and said, "That's pronounced 'plaid.'"

I was half listening, knowing the guy was at the point in the test where you had to describe a suspect's clothing.

"Yeah, what is 'plaid'?" the guy asked.

"You know, like plaid pants," the proctor said. "Plaid."

The guy kept staring up at him, like he was speaking old church Slavic.

"You know, like checks, squares," the proctor said. "The design. Plaid."

Finally, the guy got it. "Oh yeah, I always wondered what that was called," and went back to the test.

For an instant I feared that if I actually got hired, maybe I'd end up partnered with this dolt. I shook it off and went back to the test.

My results came back a few weeks later. I'd scored a 92.6. Good enough to make the first class of recruits.

A month later, the call from Applicant Investigations came through. At 12:30 A.M. on a Saturday morning. I had until the following Thursday to establish New York residency, re-register my car, obtain a New York State driver's license, and report for duty at Manhattan's Community College auditorium, downtown, for orientation. It was, I later learned, a preview to the department's philosophy of "hurry up and wait."

Through attrition, I was about to replace a cop who had retired, quit, or died. I had become part of the city's budget.

I was about to enter the machine.

THE ORGANIZATIONAL flow chart for the NYPD looks like it belongs to a Fortune 500 Company. It sprawls across the page, boxes branching off from boxes, until finally reaching the precinct-level at the bottom. When you see it for the first time you feel yourself growing smaller and smaller, realizing just how fucking huge the machinery of the department is compared to one cop.

There are more than 20,000 NYPD cops.

More than 4,080 detectives.

Two thousand sergeants.

Almost 1,200 lieutenants.

And more than 300 captains.

In total, there's over 28,000 uniformed members and more than 7,000 civilian employees. Something like 35,000 people are cashing NYPD paychecks. To get a better idea, Los Angeles only has 8,000 cops. New York has more Transit cops (more than 4,000) than Detroit has street cops.

We have more Housing Cops than New Orleans has street cops.

The NYPD's budget is over a billion—with a B— a year. And more than 90 percent of that is salary, OT, shift differential, uniform allowances, annuities, and holiday pay. The other money goes to maintaining the 1,200 RMPs, six helicopters, thirty-seven boats, twelve buses, 15,000 portable radios, a hundred horses, 80 motorcycles, 230 trucks, etc., etc., etc.

It's like working for a multi-national. Being assigned to the 7-5 is like a transfer to the branch office in Beirut. For years, in the late seventies and early eighties, the precinct was known as "Fort Fuck-Up," and some of that stigma lingers. The South Bronx may have had Fort Apache. The city even designated the original precinct house a landmark, after building the new one. But Brooklyn North had "Fort Fuck-Up," a "punishment house," where the department dumped disciplinary problems they wanted to make invisible.

When the police commissioner or mayor made one of their infrequent appearances, they'd announce the event a week in advance. It was like an inspection from the head office. We had a week to square ourselves away and organize the precinct. Then they'd walk around inattentively, nodding with bored approval, looking at nothing, before retreating back to their insulated offices at either One Police Plaza or City Hall. We wouldn't see them again until the next year, or even the year after.

What One Police Plaza wants to hear from the 7-5, or any other precinct, is numbers. Is the solvency rate for homicides up? What are the expenses? What is OT running? How many summonses are being generated? *What's the bottom line?*

That billion bucks has to come from somewhere. It comes from taxes, but also, it comes from summonses. An unspoken rule is that you write a "book" a month, minimum. A "book" consists of twenty-five summonses. Broken down that's three reds (red lights), five movers (moving violations), and seventeen parkers (parking tickets). Some sergeants, "summons hounds," will push street cops to write more and more summonses with a near-religious zeal.

Some cops write more than a book a month, tagging cars left and right. You'd think they were out

there selling Amway. Others seek out some wreck—
uninsured, unregistered and habitually illegally parked
or abandoned. Then they'll bang (multi-ticket) the shit
out of it. They'll ticket it every night. It becomes their
"summons car." It may be a derelict auto, but instead
of having it towed or "marking" it for sanitation pickup, they'll keep stuffing tickets under the wiper until
they fan out like a deck of cards. The summonses go
unpaid, but the paperwork goes through, and the precinct's numbers go up.

The cops who write the most summonses are usually
rewarded with steady seats (an RMP every night) and
few or no shit details. Those cops who don't write—
who aren't good "earners"—can expect to fly (a one-
shift detail that transfers a cop to another borough for
riot/crowd control) or walk a steady foot-post somewhere in an isolated "dead zone" of the precinct.

Yet, despite overwhelming evidence, the department
annually and categorically denies any such "summons
quota" exists. They deny it to the press again and again,
while internally they hide the fact in coded terminology
like "precinct goals" and an officer's monthly "activity."
The simple truth is, summonses generate revenue. And
revenue is good. Especially in a city like New York.

I never really liked issuing summonses. Even though
the recipients' identities remained anonymous, I was never comfortable banging (summonsing) someone. Here
was a city who demanded that cops generate revenue,
but annually refused to negotiate contract settlements
with the Patrolmen's Benevolent Association (PBA).
Cops know how much they're adding to the city's treas-
ury. It's simple arithmetic. Yet, every time a contract
expires, the negotiations turn bitter with delays, arbitration, and eventually settlements that don't even cover
cost-of-living increases.

After awhile, like a lot of cops, I got tired of it.
Every cop, every squad, every precinct spends hundreds
of thousands of hours of manpower each month, not

fighting crime, but milking a cash cow for the municipal coffers. If they were going to make us contribute to the city's parking violations franchise, then at least let us share the rewards.

Now, imagine you're a cop trying to make sense of it. The department's denials and lies. City Hall's lies and antagonism. And all around you, everyone's attitude is it's just business as usual. What do you do? You show up for roll call, hit the street, and don't think about it. Don't question it. Don't fight it. And most importantly, don't bring attention to yourself. Lose yourself in the system. The one piece of advice my OCI (official company instructor) at the Academy gave me was that "on this job, you want to remain anonymous, don't call attention to yourself and always, always CYA (Cover Your Ass)."

What he meant was, write the book a month and document everything. Don't make too many arrests, and don't make too few. And make sure your memo book is current. Whenever you tell a boss (ranking officer) something, document it. As long as somebody told someone *something* and it was documented, you're covered. As long as you're within department guidelines, you get to keep the house on Long Island, the pension, and the paycheck every two weeks.

But in truth, whatever happens out on the street really doesn't matter as long as it doesn't move upward. The rule is, never let it get as far as the sergeant, LT, CO, and then, heaven forbid, to One Police Plaza.

However, if a rumor starts spreading up through the chain of command, *everyone* tries to kill it. Crush it. Squash it. Make it disappear. And it doesn't matter if they have to sacrifice a cop to do it. Everyone is ready to serve up the person directly below them on the department's food chain. And on that chain, the cop is on the bottom.

That willingness to throw a cop away just to squash an embarrassing problem or avoid a minor scandal is known by every cop on the force. It colors his professional life, both on the street and in the precinct.

Is it any wonder there's an *us* against *them* attitude between cops and bosses, as well as the department and the city government? Is it any wonder why cops close ranks when questions are asked? Is it any wonder there's paranoia and conflict within the department? The brass against street cops. Black cops against white cops. Who is loyal? Who can be trusted to cover your back on the street? Who will sell out a partner for fear of a disciplinary loss of vacation days, transfer, or suspension?

Everyday, all over the city, cops are suspended for one week or two weeks without pay. If the reason is bad enough, they'll take the cop's gun away, issue him a "restricted" police ID, and send him to the "rubber gun squad" in some administrative purgatory. They'll try to single out one cop to hang the problem on, then make him disappear.

The higher the problems rise in the system, the more the risk to everyone who gets close to it, gets attached to it. If it rises high enough, then it becomes a political issue. And *nobody* backs up the cops. Not the brass. Not the politicians. Not the media—especially not the media. With the media, it's nothing personal, it's just that "bad cops" make "good copy." Bad cops sell papers, boost ratings, and have that ironic ring of gritty truth. A picture of a cop doing CPR on a little kid looks like a staged photo-op from the Reagan years. A cop in handcuffs, now that's urban drama.

True story. An undercover cop got into a fight with a known drug dealer, a convicted felon, and was forced to shoot him. In the aftermath former Mayor David Dinkins went and sat with the dead drug dealer's grieving family, offering his and the city's condolences. The picture is clear: The mayor is on the side of the poor community. The mayor is at odds with the PD. For cops on the job, it was a slap in the face. But for the community, it was worse. Who do *they* think runs the PD? Who does the police commissioner take his marching orders from? Who fucking appoints the police commissioner?

It's not as if the mayor and his people didn't have access to the dead drug dealer's arrest records, or the intelligence reports surrounding that particular location and the full details of the confrontation.

Maybe he was just ill-advised, but even if he wasn't, it's better to dump it on the cops—employees—than risk one degree of heat from the public.

For people who work in offices, professional politics and gossip are something to talk about at the water cooler. And if you get hit by the worst-case scenario, blind-sided, then you're looking for another job. On the street, the worst-case scenario means you're looking for another life.

You learn very quickly that the PD is run like a business. Up and down the ladder, everyone's trying to protect their jobs, build their little empires, and reach the next rung. If you're lucky, you have what used to be called a "rabbi," someone further up the ladder who can pull you up using their influence. Later, they called that person a "hook," and today he's called a "crane." But the meaning is the same, that person pulls you up from the ranks, singles you out, and sets your career on the fast track. He could be an uncle, father, or godfather, usually of the rank of captain, deputy inspector or above. Maybe years ago he was once partnered with someone now influential at One Police Plaza.

That's what all the wives and mothers want their husbands and sons eventually to become: "bosses." It shows that they're smarter than some street cop. They don't fight crime: they organize the war against it. They wear the white shirts or suits and ties, like insurance adjusters. They must be smarter. But most of all, they get to delegate authority and take the credit or distribute the blame.

When I first got to the 7-5, I was a buff. I was making two or three collars a week. Chasing down the bad guys and putting them in jail. Like a kid let loose on a life-sized movie set. Crack was king, and cops all over Brooklyn were hustling for OT. I thought I was well on my way up the ladder. I actually thought that's how you got ahead.

Ultimately, it was an exercise in futility. My efforts were recognized only by the computer that calculated the OT. The crimes and criminals themselves were blindly processed by a fragmented and overburdened judicial system.

There was something sad about all those collars. You'd catch some guy for possession and drag him downtown to BCB (Brooklyn Central Booking), then located at the rear of the 8-4 precinct.

Years ago, on a busy night, there'd be cops lining up down the stairs and out the back door with their perps. It looked like the opening night of a hit movie, except half or more than half of the people were in handcuffs. A couple of times, some lunatic in the nearby housing projects started taking pot shots at the line with a rifle. Everyone would hit the ground, perps and cops. A few minutes later, with sirens wailing in the distance, we'd stand back up, brush ourselves off, and rearrange ourselves back in line. "Hey, were you in front of me?" "Yeah." "You sure?" "I think I was in front of you."

Rain or shine, day or night, sometimes in ankle-deep snow, we'd stand outside in the lot with our perp or perps, inching our way forward. And the perps would be talking to each other, making friends. They'd discuss which cops from which precincts give the worst beatings, agreeing only on the fact that if you run, you better run fast. Because if you got caught, the cop would take it out of your ass.

Finally, we would get through the doors, up the drab stairway, and into the intake room. There, you'd photograph and fingerprint your perp before putting him into a holding cell, where he'd wait to be put on a wagon (paddy wagon) and transported to Brooklyn House of

Detention. All this before we ever saw an ADA.

This got so bad that cops, after lodging (jailing) their perps, started sacking out in any available space. The lounges, hallways, and stairwells. All hours of the day or night, you could walk up the stairs and there'd be a hundred or more cops in uniform, and plain clothes, sleeping on the floor. Cops would wipe out the precinct's vending machines of candy and sodas to the displeasure of those MOS actually stationed at the 8-4. They'd send out for pizzas and venture into Chinatown, just over the Manhattan Bridge, for Chinese food.

I remember, during the summer, you could find eight or ten cops on the roof—on the fucking roof—shirts off and sitting back in lawn chairs getting a tan. Others fashioned cots out of six water cooler jug crates, three long and two wide.

Then some scumbag infested the lounge furniture with lice and mites, adding to the friction between outside cops and 8-4 cops.

The line on the stairs created a backlog of prisoners and a dense concentration of cases that stretched through the criminal justice system to the DA's office. The ADAs were prosecuting everything, every crime. The backlog became so bad in the courts that they held what became known as "White Elephant Sales" or "Bargain Basement Days." At year's end, they'd just flush the system out. ADAs would frantically review cases, and if any looked shakey, even a little bit shakey, they'd plea the case down (lower the charges) or cut the perps free altogether. You could go down to criminal court in late December and watch two or three hundred drug dealers, muggers, crackheads, and lord knows what else, strolling out into the sunshine.

Sometime in late 1990, word of the situation threatened to hit the media just as tensions between the 8-4's cops and the rest of Brooklyn North reached the breaking point. They moved on it. And they moved fast.

In an effort that involved the DA's office, the PD, and

just about everyone else, they changed central booking for the Brooklyn North Precincts (7-3, 7-5, 7-7, 7-9, 8-1, 8-3, 9-0, and 9-4) to a more convenient and centralized location, so that it only took five or six hours to put your prisoner through the initial stages of the judicial process.

The new system, called BCAPS (Brooklyn Criminal Arrest Processing System), consists of several two-way video and voice hookups between the 8-1 Precinct, which is the new BCB, and the DA's "complaint" room, located in downtown Brooklyn. Now, you just bring your perps into the 8-1, lodge them in a temporary holding cell, then talk to an ADA on closed-circuit television. A little while later the ADA faxes back a drawn up (typed) copy of the complaint (affadavit), which the cop signs, adding rank, shield, and command, ending his tour and OT.

The new system is marginally more efficient: no more White Elephant Sales, and cop OT has been cut in half. And for a lot of cops, that means lost incentive. It's like cutting a salesman's commission. But the numbers look good for One Police Plaza. Look, crime is down! We're winning!

Reports of minor crimes *are* down. According to FBI reports, statistically Seattle has more crime than New York City. That's because people in New York City have given up reporting it. If your car gets broken into in Seattle, you call the cops. In Brooklyn, you already know the cheapest place to get the glass replaced. It's assumed the police are helpless against it. Some people get mugged and never report it. They write off the twenty or thirty bucks as a loss. They walk away thinking, "I'm damned lucky. I didn't get killed." No, they didn't get killed. But having a gun or knife put to their heads and handing over their wallet or purse isn't exactly like winning the lottery either.

All over New York, people put signs in their car windows that read, "NO RADIO" and "NOTHING IN

TRUNK." They leave these signs for criminals in the hope that a thief will read it and pass them by. That's what it's come to, leaving signs for criminals.

The thing that really gets me is this campaign they started running a couple years ago: community policing. It's an effort to put cops on foot, bringing back the old-fashioned beat cops. All over the city posters appeared in subways, on busses, and in the papers. "The Beat Cop Is Back." Stories appeared in the newspapers and on TV, where cops talked about how much they liked "getting to know the community." There was a general feeling of the old-time cop, swinging the nightstick on the end of a leather thong and rattling door handles of the local stores.

Beat cops are the wave of the future. The idea came out of a law enforcement think tank and a couple of pilot programs run by other cities.

The idea is to bring back the neighborhood cop who knows the community. Because of radios and 911 systems, response time became the determining factor in police work. Any sector car was just as good as any other. Any cop was just as good as the next. The idea was to get to the problem fast.

With community policing, the philosophy is create a presence in the neighborhood. Make those eight or ten blocks your own and enforce the law there.

But cops in precincts all over the city, and especially in places like East New York, thought, *what a fucking joke*. The only reason anybody volunteered for community policing was because they got extra chart days (days off) added to their twenty-seven annual vacation days, in addition to steady weekend RDOs. And when some cop went on television or got interviewed, they knew exactly what to say. All those interviews were weirdly alike, with every single cop using practically the same words to describe the program.

In a lot of precincts, community policing cops are

tokens, thrown out on the street to write summonses, look sharp, and create a sense of public security through *omnipresence*.

The department wants it like it used to be, only different. Up until the sixties and seventies, cops on the beat were still accepting "Christmas envelopes" from store owners and residents. If a cop went into a candy store for a soda, he'd put the money on the counter with his soft drink and the store owner would put the soda in the bag, the straw in the bag, and the cop's money in the bag before handing it back across the counter to him. That's the way it was done. Then, there are the stories you hear from the past about young widows, and lonely wives on cold wintery nights.

It's as American as Norman Rockwell's *Saturday Evening Post* cover of the cop boosting an apple from the green grocer's. Today, that wouldn't work. Do you take the free cup of coffee? Do you take the free coffee and donut? Do you take the free lunch? How about the free steak dinner? What about the envelope at Christmas?

That Norman Rockwell cop on the beat had a personal relationship with all the store owners and was respected by the community. There was this very human factor in it. He knew who the bad eggs were, and he knew how to keep them in line: back at the precincts they actually had rubber hoses and water-soaked phone books. If a store was broken into, they would round up the five worst guys they could find and beat the living shit out of them, one after another, until one of them confessed or ratted the perp out.

Those were the days of the beat cop giving some smart-ass kid a swift kick in the ass. It was the days of the cop hauling a kid by the ear back home to have a talk with his parents. If you did either of those things today, you'd either have the CCRB (Civilian Complaint Review Board) so far up your ass you couldn't breathe or the smart-ass kid would come back and take a shot at you with a nine millimeter semiautomatic, because you dissed him. Not to mention the innumerable "excessive force" lawsuits filed every year.

Proponents of community policing want something more wholesome than the *Saturday Evening Post* and Norman Rockwell. And they want it in places like East New York. They want to play a Frank Capra movie for the public. But that movie doesn't play in the ghetto. In the ghetto, it would be like watching one of those Japanese films where the voices are out of sync with the movement of the actors' mouths.

In midtown, you could put beat cops on every corner to answer questions from tourists and chase away the guys selling bogus Rolexes out of plastic briefcases. And it would work. It does work: in midtown. The store owners like it and the tourists find out how to get to the Empire State Building.

But the people who live in East New York, who read the stories in the papers or watch the news on television, say, "Bullshit! Who do they think they're fooling with that lame crap?" Who they're fooling is the white, middle class, liberal, voting public who has never been, and never wants to go into, the ghetto.

The community policing cop isn't going to run into a drug shoot-out in a housing project—that's Housings' (Housing PD) job, where an RMP cop with a partner would run in. The community policing cop isn't going to handle a domestic dispute without calling for backup. And community policing doesn't work midnights. In East New York a lot of midnight cops won't even stop at red lights or stop signs, because they've been shot at one too many times while sitting at one.

The community policing cop is going to walk around during the day, presenting a professional image for $45,000 a year, waiting for another reporter to show up.

We've gone beyond the point where we can ever go back to the way it was. The system is different. Criminals are different. The world is different. The balance of fear on the street has shifted. In reality, the department doesn't even want to go back to the way it used to be. Because out of those free cups of coffee, free meals, and envelopes at Christmas grew a cancerous, virulent corruption. The coffee became an expected perk. The meals became plentiful. And the envelopes didn't just come from shop owners. They started coming from bookies, pimps, and drug dealers. And they fucking well were expected—every week.

Even the term "tenderloin," came from the "old" NYPD. Back in the late 1800s the notorious police captain, Alexander "Clubber" Williams, was transferred from the poor neighborhood of the Fourth Precinct, to the crime-ridden 29th Precinct.

The move suited Williams perfectly. Filled with whorehouses, saloons, thieves, and other Victoriana vices, the 29th covered an area from 14th Street to 42nd Street, and from Fifth Avenue to Seventh Avenue. Ground zero was Sixth Avenue and Thirtieth Street.

He filled the station house with the meanest cops he could find, then said after living on rump roast for so long, he could now afford to "eat tenderloin." He's the guy who also said, "There is more law in the end of a policeman's nightstick than in a decision of the Supreme Court."

So much for the good ol' days.

Everybody's always talking about corrupt cops. The way the newspapers and television shows make it seem, every cop in the NYPD is accepting money and dealing drugs.

Watching the Mollen Commission, a special corruption hearing board, in progress, cops throughout the city couldn't believe it. "Rogue" cops picking up drug dealers off the street, then delivering them to a rival gang to get whacked. Cops dealing drugs—stealing drugs— through an RMP window!

The whole thing was like some bizarre, alternate universe. The public may have been shocked, but cops all over New York were watching these hearings with dismay, their jaws dropped open. These guys were cops. COPS. What in the name of Christ happened to them?

All over the city, good cops must've been asking themselves some hard questions. Is this the way it starts, by taking a free soda? Is the free coffee the first domino? Is it like a disease that gets worse and worse?

And yet, on some level, it does make sense. Because in the ghetto, nothing much seems to matter. The drugs will be there anyway. The guns will be there anyway. Every cop knows that—but these guys slipped way over the line in their thinking. They not only took on the camouflage of the street—they became the street. They slid down to the level of the scumbags—perps. And when they did that, they disrespected not only themselves, but the uniform, the department, and the badge as well. They made it that much harder for every uniformed cop on the street to receive the respect we've earned.

Bosses, sergeants, LTs, captains, and COs have thousands of ways to punish a cop—none of them written down in the Patrol Guide. And that's the difference between punishment and discipline. You can be punished for anything; not writing enough summonses, not answering radio calls, or just for having a "bad attitude." It's made worse by the fact that punishments are unofficial, there's nobody to talk to about it.

Cops that want out of a precinct can get hammered (punished) night after night with "punishment posts": fixer/posts guarding EDPs (emotionally disturbed persons) or prisoners, until they "shape up" or surrender and put in a "57" (request for transfer).

Sometimes cops almost wish the CO would just "give them one," a CD (command discipline). An official punishment that results in a cop "losing a day" (forfeiture of a vacation day) or a lesser action of two, four, or even

six hours of pay. But because of the way the department is structured, they have to justify these measures.
By hammering a cop with a shit detail or a bad foot-
post, bosses don't have to justify anything. They just
put the cop on it. It can make your life miserable. You
can find yourself in hot humid weather, wearing a bulletproof vest, sweating your balls off, walking a "beat in
the heat." Or freezing your ass off with not much protection against the elements.

I've seen cops who've had "attitude problems" walking a foot post in some "dead zone" of the precinct,
turned into an unofficial "square badge" by a spiteful
LT with a chip on his shoulder.

Being put on an EDP at King's County Hospital means
sitting in the "G" building (psych ward) all night, while
the attending physician debates the prisoner's condition
and whether to admit or release him. Basically, it's a
demeaning babysitting job.

I've gotten hammered a few times for some minor
violation (uniform infraction). And I learned quickly
that there are ways to make the best of a bad situation.
You learn these lessons from other cops or people who
just happened to be around.

If you're in a sector car, courtesy warrants you go
around to the foot posts, watching out for the guys
"doing their time." You bring them food or coffee. If
it's a cold night and the LT isn't on the ball, then you
put the cop in the backseat of the RMP and drive him
around for the remainder of the tour, making him the
third man in the car.

Probably the best kept secret of all the shit details
is "sitting on" (guarding) an injured prisoner admitted
to the hospital. When the prisoner's too out of it or
drugged with painkillers, cops will call down to the
desk and have his television and telephone hooked up.
The only thing left to do then is search the halls for a
comfortable chair, talk food services into a free meal,
and try to make a date with any available nurses. Gen-

erally you make yourself at home, sit back, and watch the late movie eating green Jell-O.

But one time in probationary police officer training, I was assigned to the psych ward of Bellevue Hospital in Manhattan, guarding a prisoner, while a cop from another precinct was guarding his prisoner. I was sitting there, watching TV, when I noticed that the other cop's prisoner was scratching himself with his right hand across his throat real quick, with jerky movements. I just figured, well, the guy's a nutcase. Probably hallucinating insects or something.

After he did this three or four times, I noticed a thin trickle of blood starting to bead down his chest. I panicked for an instant, then I saw the edge of a razorblade between his fingers.

I was out of my chair and over the edge of the prisoner's wheelchair in a heartbeat, the other cop right behind me. I grabbed the guy's hand at the wrist, while the other cop tried to pry the rusty razorblade from between the guy's fingers. It took a full half minute before we managed to get the blade out of his hand. Then we got one of the nurses to clean him up. Luckily the wounds on his neck were only superficial. The other cop was grateful. Shit, if anything had happened to his prisoner, that cop would never have seen the street again—being caught forever in some twilight zone of punishment post after punishment post.

But shit details never seem to end, especially when a boss flies (sends) you out to some riot, protest, or "precinct condition" in another part of the city. New York is the fucking land of protests. Everyone who has a beef with the city, state, or federal government launches a protest. The minute someone in New York gets a permit to demonstrate or causes a disturbance, it costs the city money and inconveniences the public.

The clearest memory I have of this is sitting in a police van in Manhattan with five other cops on a rainy day. It was the World Trade Center Bombing detail. We just sat there for hours, securing the perimeter, while this rookie sergeant, who was originally a Manhattan task force cop, went on about what a great place the city was. "That's the great thing about Manhattan," he said. "You know, you could see anyone, Robert DeNiro, Al Pacino, or someone." He went on about it for hours, naming every movie star he'd ever seen. A true stargazer. After eight hours of this verbal torture, the driver started the van and drove us back to Brooklyn, back home to the ghetto.

But the worst, the absolute worst, is guarding a corpse. If a boss really fucking hates you, he'll single you out and put you on a stiff, waiting for the ME (medical examiner) to come and remove the body. One minute you could be in a sector car, cruising along, and the next thing you know you're "on a DOA," standing around in some illegal basement apartment watching over some old person who's been dead for three, four, or five days. Inevitably the body's turning pretty ripe, and you can smoke all the cigars and put all the mentholatum you want under your nose, but it won't help. If you're lucky, someone's thrown a sheet over them, but that doesn't always happen. And it could take anywhere from two to five hours before the ME's van shows up.

What it comes down to is that the bosses can screw up your life, big time, and unofficially. That's the scary part: that it's unofficial, which means it's personal. And that's why a lot of cops feel trapped between the street and the precinct.

I had just finished seven months training at the Academy and was to report to the 13th Precinct, just around the corner. The 13th Precinct was the borough command of Manhattan South. It was also NSU #2 (neighborhood stabilization unit/probationary training) Central Command. Back then, NSU was a program that provided added police presence in problem areas citywide. It was like temp help for the precincts, drawing on a pool of rookie manpower. But is also allowed PPOs (probationary police officers) to get a taste of everything. Law enforcement dim sum.

I was still a PPO, but had gained experience from Greenwich Village, the East Village, Hell's Kitchen, and Grammercy Park.

Walking the beat, I'd chased hookers, busted street peddlers, and collared drug dealers. Like other newly released recruits put onto the street, I threw myself into it, getting involved every chance I could.

As a squad, we were assigned an experienced sergeant and depending on the sergeant and the other PPOs you could get involved as much as you wanted. A lot of the squad sergeants, I'm sure, just wanted to sit back and relax: not taking (answering calls) from the precinct's assigned frequency. And here they were matched up with newly graduated academy recruits, eager PPOs. Depending on whether they saw their PPOs as shakey or not, they'd play along. It was a lot like letting little kids play with the police siren.

Fortunately, I had a couple of good mentors and managed to get involved quite a bit. This other PPO and I led our squad in arrests.

I'd been on the job about a year and thought I'd seen it all. I'd been in four Manhattan South Precincts. Four! I'd survived the worst of the East Village, alphabet city. And worked its drug cleanup effort, called Operation Pressure Point. I thought I was tough enough for anything New York had to offer.

When it came time to be assigned to a permanent command, my father handed me this business card of an associate of his. Apparently this associate's brother was a NYPD captain. He suggested I call the associate and have the associate call his brother to have a good word put in and maybe the captain could "hook me up." Like everywhere else in New York, it seemed, it was a matter of who you knew.

I looked at the card for a long time, then made the

call. He was cordial and was willing to go out of his way to help me out.

"What do you want out of this job?" he asked.

"I want to get the most experience as fast as possible," I remember saying. "I want an 'A' House" ("heavy"/busy precinct).

A week later, I'd talked to the 13th Precinct's PBA delegate. He asked me the same thing.

"Just give me the worst area they have here," I said. They both told me the same thing.

"You want an 'A' House . . ."

"You want experience . . ."

"You want exposure . . ."

" . . . Go to the 7-5."

"Then that's where I want to go," I told both of them. The 7-5 became like a goal. But as it turned out, you didn't need a "hook" to get sent there.

Most of the cops there were looking for a "hook" to get out.

15

NIGGERS.

Fucking niggers.

Motherfucking niggers.

I've been spit on by little kids.

Cursed out by teenage mothers.

Been called "cracker" by criminals.

And every night—every fucking night—I've gotten those long stares, filled with challenge and hate, by the very people I'm sworn to protect. How can you respect or protect people who hate you? Who hate your very presence.

What do you want to know about racial tension in the ghetto? East New York is mostly African-American and Hispanic. The majority of cops on patrol there are white. What more do you *need* to know? We are divided by skin color, economics, and lifestyle. The police in the 7-5 are an occupying force, far removed from its residents.

We are the white faces in the blue-and-white cars. *We* are the outsiders, the interlopers, and the authority that is not always fair or benign. You might get smacked for copping an attitude when an officer pulls your car over and tosses (searches) it for a gun. You might get shot for reaching too quickly toward the glove box for your registration. You might get called a *nigger*, *hamster*, *skell*, *bone*, or *scumbag* just for hanging out in front of your own house.

164

"Get out the car! Put your fucking hands on the hood! I don't wanna hear a fuckin' word from you. Nothing!"

Night after night I've gone into homes of people who have the least in our society. I've gone into their living rooms, bathrooms, and bedrooms. I've seen the shabbiness, the cheapness, the hopelessness of their lives. I've seen it and it's vile.

In their own homes, they tell us detailed stories while displaying their wounds. They show us their grief, anger, and shame. Oddly, it doesn't make them more human, because most of us in the 7-5 have seen it too often. For us there is no story, no grief, no wound that is not included in the Penal Law. Every horror, tragedy, and indignity matches the numbered paragraphs and its subdivisions the Penal Code.

As ghetto cops we bare witness to the worst imaginable crimes: knowing that most are committed by black males between the ages of 15 to 25. Thousands of crimes and hundreds of arrests—all age 15 to 25. If you're shot in the ghetto, the odds say that a black male between 15 and 25 pulled the trigger. Yes, black, mostly black, but also the shooter could be P.R. (Puerto Rican), Columbian, or Dominican. These are the facts.

"Listen you fuckin' nigger, I hear another word outta you, I'm gonna tune (beat) your ass! Understood?"

Every cop wants to go home at the end of their tour. It's always better to be safe than sorry. You're a fucking criminal until the cop knows differently.

If you're a black male between 15 and 25, cops come down on you, hard. They curse you. Harass you. Maybe even hit you. In our eyes you're a potential felon. You look like a felon. Maybe you'll do a crime in the future. Maybe you won't. You may be an honest decent human being. The *statistics say that you probably are*—most 15 to 25 year olds aren't out doing crimes. But when you're a cop, it genuinely seems otherwise. The *statistics* say there's a good chance you might not be.

"Whose car is this? Where do you live? Where the fuck're you going, huh? Don't turn 'round to look at me! Look at the fucking hood! What are you doing in my neighborhood, huh?"

My neighborhood. Mine. Not possessed with pride or maintained with care, but by necessity. Owned only by force and the mandate of law.

For eight hours and thirty-five minutes a day each tour inherits the squalor and violence. Even the dead and the crime scenes are part of our domain. We are the ones who witness and chronicle the daily terrors of the ghetto, working against the tide by force and presence. And seeing hope only at the end of the commute home to a very different kind of ownership.

"You live here? You live in this fucking shit-hole? No? What're you doin here, huh? What're you doing 'round here this time of night, huh?"

Don't expect an apology either. Because all the cursing, harassing, shoulder throwing, attitude, and the rest of it, none of it's personal—at least not from the ghetto cop's standpoint. You're a statistic, a profile. And it's better to suspect and be wrong, than be foolish and dead. There's a saying in the NYPD that helps us to justify our actions in the street and define our suspicions: "Better to be judged by twelve, than carried by six." Taking the time to decipher good guy from bad, perp from bystander, can cost you a split-second decision that could have saved your life.

So how can Blacks and Hispanics respect the authority that does not respect them? Nor act fairly and justly on their behalf? What faith can they put in a *system* that preaches innocence, but assumes guilt? The same system created by a society that makes them, and other minorities, recipients of contemptuous neglect.

The results: fear on both sides, hate on both sides, and guns on both sides.

What more do you need to know? That's the *reality*.

It's bigger than just one cop in the ghetto. It's bigger than an entire police department. The hatred, suspicion, bigotry, and contempt is embedded in minds so deep that nothing can dislodge it.

But don't you dare judge the ghetto cop. If you're white and living in the suburbs, don't judge him before looking into your own heart and examining your own fears. Whatever chatter you have ready for a cocktail party, bar, or water cooler, you are *not* on the street in the ghetto. You aren't a part of it, and you hope with every fiber of your soul that you never take that wrong turn that puts you there.

If you're black and living *anywhere*, don't you judge the ghetto cop before examining your own shame. If you're black, honest, and hard-working, what secret shame do you possess at every news broadcast or every turn of a newspaper's page? What secret prayer of *"please, don't make him African-American,"* do you repeat silently to yourself?

All the antecedents, theories, history, well-reasoned rules of decency, and politically correct *New York Times* editorials aren't worth shit on the street. History is past tense, theories may be wrong, and the editorial writers do not live in the ghetto. Everything on the street is immediate.

For everyday of a cop's life—every tour in his career—the street is an overwhelming reality. That moment you push through a door, approach the driver of a car, and walk up a housing project's narrow stairwell is overwhelming. The present drowns out everything. In the ghetto, in a place where kindness is often mistaken for weakness, nobody wants to gamble their life on manners.

In the ghetto—on the street—precious little is polite. Courtesy is a luxury. Subtlety is a meaningless concept. There is no code for the hate and fear on both sides. It's taken for granted. Trust no one, suspect everyone. Caution is a survival skill—paranoia the instinct to survive.

Nobody pretends it doesn't exist. The way it feels is nearly tangible—like something you could touch or see.

There's no mystery to the "*us and them*" mentality of the street. There is no mystery to survival.

We are becoming a divided nation of us and thems. We are becoming a nation of tribes, gangs, enclaves, or whatever other name you want to put to it.

But don't you dare judge the ghetto cop.

Judge Manhattan. Stand out on Sixth Avenue and 53rd Street. Every weekday from nine in the morning it's one of the most densely populated areas of the city. At 5:00 P.M. all those buildings vomit out hordes of comfortably white office workers—walking fast for The Port Authority, Grand Central, and Penn Station.

It's a sea of white faces contrasting dark suits and ties heading to commuter trains on tight schedules that will take them back to the comfort of a safe, expensive American dream. If you see a black face, it's usually a messenger, a kid that works in the mailroom, a secretary, a street vendor—or the unacknowledged homeless picking through the trash for lunch hour soda cans. Is that a coincidence? It's not a secret. It's there for everyone to see.

If you're a black male between the ages of 15 and 25 walking around midtown, you'd have to be blind not to see that very few of those people, those hundreds of thousands of people, look like you. Who could help but think those offices weren't built for you to work in. Those jobs weren't created for you to do. Those suits and ties, coffee breaks, and corporate lunches, they ain't for you. You want to make some money? Learn to play a sport, start a rap group . . . or deal drugs. Two long shots, and a fast way to get capped (killed). Those are the career options.

People living in public housing are forced to rent mail drops when they apply for jobs, fearing their addresses will disqualify them.

Employment agencies and personnel departments write "All American" on job applications to denote "white." They speak in polite code and go home every night thinking they are good and decent people who work among other good and decent people. The truth is too ugly for them. The racism is subtly and politely coded. Even to acknowledge—to mention it—is at best to exhibit bad taste. To say the words out loud is to cross a line and admit something themselves.

Real estate agents know where to take prospective tenants of color. As if to say, "We may be elitist, but we are Afro-American friendly." Bullshit! The only gullible idiot that'd buy into that pitch would be some submissive or demoralized Uncle Tom.

If you want to stop crime, violence, and make a cop's job easier, find these people jobs.

Go into any expensive restaurant, elite hotel, or posh shop. White. White. White. If you see a black face, ninety-nine times out of a hundred it belongs to a minimum-wage busboy, chambermaid, or security guard.

Better yet—become the black 17-year-old male in midtown and wander into an expensive store. What you get is a floor walker following your black ass around the instant you push through the revolving doors. You're a suspect, a criminal the moment you enter. You look like a fucking criminal. You look like the picture in the paper of a guy in cuffs. *You're a profile.*

What about black cops?

I have seen them on countless occasions coming in through the back door of the precinct with a black suspect in handcuffs. They come through that door out of a darkened parking lot and into the fluorescent glare, and it is sad. It's sad beyond large important words like tragic and heroic. To think that the best way they can do their job and serve the people is to lock up their people.

I didn't know much about what black cops thought. I honestly didn't think about it.

I remember sitting in a patrol car one night with one of my old partners. She's a good cop: tough, smart, fair, and black.

We were sitting in the shadows on New Jersey Avenue just off Pitkin Avenue, shooting the shit and talking about how Brooklyn was rioting over in the 71st Precinct, Crown Heights. It was a tense time. The city defined more than usual by black and white, specifically, Jews and Blacks. The division also cut straight into the heart of the police department.

I remember asking her, "Brenda what would you do? If it had come down to it? What would you do if you had to choose sides?" What I meant was, if it was between me and some black guy on the street, in a life or death situation. But she knew what I meant.

Brenda had been "on the job" for over ten years. She had known, grown with, and dealt with racism here, long before I arrived in 7-5. She's had to contend with social bias, racial bias, gender bias, and the culmination of all three: professional bias.

I knew very little about her personal life, but what I did know made me respect her. At eighteen she got pregnant and had a daughter. The father split. At twenty she joined the PD, and put her time in on patrol and in "details" at various precincts. As a black female and single mother employed by a department that professes "we're all blue," but practices subtle gender and racial biases, she had an uphill struggle.

Years later, here she was in the 7-5. The armpit of NYC. Patrolling a neighborhood, and people, she probably would rather not. Sitting in an RMP, partnered up with some "white-bread" cop, displaced in the ghetto. "My lord," she'd always say. But she was honest. A little cautious sometimes with her words, but honest.

I usually knew where she was coming from. How she felt and what opinions she held on controversial subjects. This was one of them. But, I wasn't uncomfortable asking those questions. They had to be asked not just for my safety, but for both our safety.

"I'm a cop," she said. "But if you ever did anything to dishonor this uniform or blatantly engage in a racially motivated manner, I'd have to go with what I believe. You got to understand, I won't be a hypocrite and I won't stand by and witness an unprovoked assault because of skin color. Fair enough?"

"Fair enough," I thought. She was right, it was fair enough. However, she also knew Crown Heights was a fucking melee. Cops with hats and bats (riot helmets and nightsticks). Hasidim out in force, no weapons. And blacks, armed with Molotov cocktails, guns, bottles, and anything else projectable.

I also made it very clear to her where I stood if by chance we ended up being flown or mobilized (sent to other precincts) to the 7-1. If attacked by a rushing crowd of angry black youths, fucking-a-right I'd wield a heavy stick. At that point *they* do become *niggers*. Not out of ingrained prejudice, bigotry, or racism, but out of passion and survival. When threatened and outnumbered, survival by any means is your only rationale. Especially as a cop, especially as a human being.

But that's not the heart of it. If you're a black cop working in the ghetto, you must feel the pain. Maybe you came from a place like East New York. Maybe you still have family there. And, after all, these are still *your people*. The people who know what it means to live in a place like New York City as a black person. There's a bond.

But every day, day in and day out, you must see your own people suffering. You see it without the benefit of "us" and "them." You see it closer, feel it more. Sharing a measure of the despair and disparity in a socially unequal place.

Up until I became a cop in New York City, I didn't know or even think about what black people thought. Why did I have to? Why did I have to care about a group of people whose culture I was never going to embrace or have to live in? Typical attitude for an upper-middle-class, preppy white boy from Shaker Heights, Ohio: a kid who grew up spending summers on caucasian Cape Cod, sailing, swimming, and sunning.

Except for an occasional trip through "bad" neighborhoods to get to Cleveland's Municipal Stadium to see a Browns game, my universe consisted of green lawns and large Georgian homes. Those "trips" downtown, through "bad" areas, provided a geography lesson in where not to go. The sight of prostitutes along Cleveland's Prospect Avenue and 30th Street, the Hough Projects and the infamous Greyhound Bus Terminal on Chester Avenue, home to transients, social misfits, and pimps. As a sheltered child I grouped them all as one. They represented a threat, and clearly that is what my parents intended them to be for me. These were the landmarks of the lower class: undesirable, uncomprehensible, and above all dangerous.

The people who inhabited these places were there by choice, because of some grave defect, or maybe even sin. I remember passing by some projects and tenements along West Cleveland's Woodhill Avenue and Hough Avenue, this raised my curiosity. Seeing boarded up windows, spray-painted graffiti, and garbage strewn across courtyards—questions lingered. Who lives there? I don't live like that. Who does? And the response was always the same. Black people. Black people live there.

IT WAS one of those nights that just seemed to go on forever. Each step moved us downward a notch on the respectability scale as we became drunker, stupider, and now patently unlawful. There wasn't a sober guy in the car, even the driver.

Then suddenly, the world seemed to explode. The muzzle flash was blinding. The shot rang out in the small car, numbing my ears as the business section of Queens Boulevard flew by us. The gunshot, not a foot away, sent me back against the seat, leaving me shaking my head and blinking away the purple spots from the muzzle flash, as the smell of gunpowder filled the car.

"Fuck!"

"What the fuck?"

And all along, the cop in the front seat was laughing because he'd just "capped off" spontaneously through the moonroof. Regaining my sight, and realizing what he'd done, I quickly scanned the vicinity for an RMP who might have seen us. None in sight.

I was in the second of three or four cars filled with off-duty cops, moving along Queens Boulevard. All night the caravan moved from one titty bar to the next, as if in the next one the girls would be more beautiful, more provocative, more . . . something.

In the last couple of years, all these topless bars had sprung up around Manhattan, Queens, and Brooklyn.

Stringfellows, Pure Platinum, Gold Fingers, Dallas Gold. Not the run down, seedy topless bars of old, these were upscale places that charged a cover and then charged four or five bucks a beer. They were a regular phenomenon in the age of AIDS. They took credit cards and were popular among the corporate set. Much of their business came from expense account money, charged on corporate American Express cards. Their interiors were polished brass and mirrors illuminated by stage and strobe lights. The women who danced were not only beautiful, but said to make three, four, or five hundred dollars a night. All of this was supposed to make these joints *respectable*. But really, they were just the same old places, repackaged.

So far that night we'd been to five or six of them— tinning (flashing badges) our way in, never paying the cover—and staying in each one just long enough to buy two or three rounds.

Now we were thoroughly drunk and on our way to the last stop. Wylie's, in Jackson Heights.

"You're gonna love this place," one of the cops said. "Love it."

Finally, we got there to find a bar without a sign or front window. The steel door had a sliding peephole, like a speakeasy. After one of the guys provided the right password, the door opened and we trooped in.

Inside, three or four guys sat hunched over their beers, and a Spanish woman danced naked on a small stage at the rear of the bar. Three or four more women, Spanish, black and Oriental, stood around the perimeter, sizing up our group.

The deal was "lap-dancing," where the women would come over and for a continued flow of five-dollar bills sit on your lap, grinding away in simulated screwing as you fondled her breasts and genitals.

I'd passed the point of comfortably drunk several rounds ago, but ordered a beer anyway. I found a seat in the back and the women started approaching me, one after another. When it became clear I wasn't interested in lap-dancing, they stopped approaching. A couple of the women were already grinding down on a few of the other guys.

It took about twenty minutes for the situation to start getting out of hand. One of the guys bet that he'd eat an after dinner mint out of one of the women for twenty-five bucks. A collection was taken up, while negotiations were being made with the dancer.

When I saw one of the other cops leave the bar, I followed him out, knowing he was drunker than I was. I found him outside, pissing against an alley wall.

"What the fuck are we doing here?" I asked him.

But before he could answer, glass broke at the far end of the alley, and this guy climbed out the window holding a VCR.

"What the fuck?" the other cop said, reaching for his gun.

Somewhere off in the distance there was a shot.

"You gonna go after him?" the other cop said.

"Fuck, no."

"Let's go back inside."

"Fuck no, let's get out of here."

On a young department like this, a lot of cops act like kids. They graduate high school, join the force as soon as they turn twenty, and that's it. They're expected to be role models, pillars of the community, "good boys" twenty-four, seven, three-six-five.

Plus, in a precinct like the 7-5, you're in a pressure cooker for eight and a half hours a day. And sometimes the only thing you have to unwind is a cold one or whatever minor vices are available.

Sometimes you see cops after their tours drinking out in the MOS lot by their cars. They gather in bars. They go on binges. And when an alcohol problem develops, they go to "the farm," an NYPD facility upstate for intensive counseling or "brainwashing," as they say around the precincts.

But it makes you wonder, just how much OT ends up in places like Stringfellows or Gold Fingers?

There isn't a bar in New York that'll stop a cop at the door and charge him a cover. Topless joints welcome cops with open arms. Not only is an off-duty cop capable of making infinite trouble for the management by phoning in a bogus "13" just to fill the place full of uniforms. But cops who will stop the newspaper delivery truck at three in the morning for a free paper will spend cash like a drunken sailor in those places.

It also makes you wonder how many excuses are given to wives and girlfriends. Sometimes the excuses seem infinite. I've sat behind the desk, assigned to the TS (telephone switchboard) answering the phone. If it's a wife asking about her husband, there's an SOP (standard operating procedure).

"Is Bob Smith there? This is his wife."

Bob Smith's tour ended three hours ago and he's probably out getting shit-faced with his squad, but the officer on the TS should always answer, "One moment please, I'll check the roll-call sheet."

Then you keep her on hold for awhile. The new wives will lose patience and hang up. Older ones will hang in there. Then you get back on and say, "He's made a collar, he's probably down at BCB—it should be awhile."

Some of the wives who know their husbands and know they couldn't "find a collar in a shirt factory" will thank you and then bitch him out when he gets home.

Other times, the wife will call *before* the husband's shift ends and say, "You tell him straight home after work."

As far as I can see, the wives' paranoia can be pretty well-founded. These guys get married young: 22, 24, or 25. And one day, like a lot of guys who marry young, they wake up and feel they're missing something. That something, nine times out of ten, is more women. And if you're a cop, it's easier to rationalize: *Hell, I could be killed any time. I deserve this.*

The wives know it. They can feel it. When cops get together with their families, you'll see all the cops standing around, a beer in their hands, talking about work—"the job." And off to the side, there will be the wives, gathered in a tight little group. They'll be talking about kids and houses, but also, the older wives will be sharing information with the younger ones. The older ones schooling the young ones on all the excuses, so that by the time the rookie makes his first excuse for getting home at four in the morning, the wife is already wise to it.

And the husbands, they know the one rule: Deny it, when faced with solid evidence: deny it. *Deny. Deny. Deny.* The harder the evidence, the stronger the denial. But deny it, whatever it is. Denial raises doubt. And as long as you have that one small grain of doubt, then you're home free.

The one exception, of course, is the wife or girlfriend who is also a cop. She knows all the angles. She's heard the denials. She also knows the job. And she's not going to buy into any of it.

The flip side of it is, that on weekends or RDOs, a lot of cops will work like dogs, laboring not only on their own houses, but those of their friends as well. Within the force, there's this huge talent pool of cops who can do drywalling, carpentry, electrical work, plumbing, you name it. Maybe their fathers did it for a living or they picked it up on summer jobs during high school. However it happened, from this cop community of talent an informal barter system arose. Additions to houses, dens, decks, and in one case I know of, a beauty parlor was constructed out of this off-duty work force.

This is *our* form of escapism, our way of decompressing and winding down away from work. These guys will show up at their friend's home with toolbelts, power-saws, sanders, and whatever other tools they need, like an old-fashioned barn raising, and go to work.

*   *   *

Callahan's is basically an old-fashioned bar dressed up with a new interior. It's the bar where "the system" unwinds. On any given Friday, there'll be ADAs, public defenders, cops, court officers, lawyers, and judges spread out over its three rooms.

Not surprisingly, there isn't much intermingling until four or five drinks have been consumed. Then, you're likely to see the young female legal aide attorney wandering back into enemy territory to chat with a male ADA. A little later, you'll see the detective discreetly leave five minutes ahead of either an ADA, paralegal, or legal aide attorney, only to hook up later at either one's apartment.

Maybe the bosses and supervisors of these offices would be surprised, but all these inter-office liaisons make perfect sense. Everyone's underpaid and overworked. Everyone's hours are crazy. Everyone needs to unwind. And everyone wants to talk about their work, or not talk about their work, or get laid. If you're involved in the system, you know the work, know the horrors, know the system.

Say you're a legal aide lawyer defending some guy who murdered three people, execution style, during a drug transaction. You tell that to a date, someone *outside* this circle, like an advertising executive from Manhattan, and there's a good chance they'll run screaming from the room. There's a good chance you're not going to get lucky that night.

Or, suppose you're a cop, and you're two hours late for a date because you had to secure some crime scene. If you're dumb enough to tell her or him *why* you were late, you might get, *"Oh, murder, how interesting . . ."* Then you start giving out facts. Like maybe it was a 16 year old, gunned down for a jacket, sneakers, or necklace, and suddenly it's a whole lot less interesting. It's pathetic and sad beyond words. But most of all, your date wants to know why this particular death doesn't have you sobbing into your entree or ranting against social injustices. *Why hasn't it rocked your world?*

It hasn't rocked your world because there was the infant last week who was left in the trash bin and the innocent kid who was caught in the cross fire the week before and died. Or the accident victim of a drunk driver the week before that. And all of a sudden, you're not the fun, interesting date he or she thought you might have been when they spoke to you over the phone.

But if you told something like that to an ADA, public defender, or another cop, they wouldn't be shocked. They'd understand it. They'd understand, that's your job. And they'll understand that you have maybe one night a week to see them. Because whether you're a cop, ADA or legal aide attorney, you're buried under cases and case files.

The relationships within the system aren't much, cordial if not convenient. Everyone's heard the stories, the gossip. But really, the gossip isn't all that interesting, who took whom to the Kew Motor Inn in Queens, "Where Romance Is Always in Bloom," featuring fourteen different room themes—including Egyptian, Safari, and Arabian Nights. No reservations.

In the end it's just clothesline gossip. These couples become an item for a week, a month, for six months, then drift apart. Very rarely, almost never, do you ever hear about them marrying or moving in together. And very rarely does anyone care why it ended. Only the fact that it ended seems of consequence. Everyone is interested in the final disposition—the sentencing, not the verdict.

But they do end. Most of the time they seem half-ended before they've begun. Not ill-fated, but simply following the rules of procedure. They are nearly all predictably short-lived within the grinding mechanism of the criminal justice machine and the random bullshit of the street.

They end more like departmental or office transactions than like love affairs.

There are stray dogs roaming all over East New York. Some of them are pets people have turned lose, others have been born out on the street. They've turned feral, adapting to their environment, and somehow surviving. In a lot of ways, they're perfect creatures of the environment. Nobody pays any attention to them. They wander, day and night through the streets, part of the landscape and population.

Sometimes they travel in packs, sometimes alone. They're all just a little taller than knee-height, and are for the most part all mutts. And when you see them, you can sometimes pick out the different breeds. You see the collie-shepherd, Doberman-shepherd, or retriever-shepherd. The shepherd features are always prominent.

One night, we were lined up for roll call, when a four-to-midnight cop, Eric Chapman, brought in this dog and started asking around if anyone wanted it. It caused kind of a minor disruption at the desk, but no takers. After a little while, Chapman took off for the locker room and they coaxed the dog back out into the night.

When roll call was dismissed, I headed out to the back lot with my partner and grabbed an RMP. By this time it started to rain.

We were about five blocks from the precinct when I caught sight of something out of the corner of my eye, just a shadow, moving fast into the street from the curb.

I jammed on the brakes and brought the car to a skidding stop. It was that dog again. She stood there for an instant, caught in the headlights, all skin and bone.

"What the fuck?" my partner said.

"It's that dog, the one Chapman brought in."

"Yeah, so."

I reached around and opened the rear door to the RMP. The dog trotted around the front of the car and jumped in, sat down, and shook-off the water all over us and the car.

"What the fuck you doing?" my partner asked.

"I'm gonna keep it," I answered, not really thinking about it until I said it.

"What? It's a fucking ghetto dog."

"Fucking right," I said.

"You're a fucking EDP, that's a ghetto dog. Why don't you get something nice?"

"Fuck that, I'm gonna keep it," I said adamantly. Probably taking on more that I realized.

She may have been free, but she cost a shitload in vet bills and a lot more just to fatten her up, so at least she would look like something. The vet, as close as he could tell, categorized her pedigree as part huskie and part *wolf*.

That wolf part probably included some shepherd as well; for years people have been breeding shepherds with wolves, using them as protective pets and for security work.

From the first time I saw her, there was this wild aspect to her movements and appearance. That quality remains today, untempered by domestication. I ended up calling her Dakota.

My whole life, I was raised with pure-bred dachshunds—suburban hounds—but this dog is the best I've ever had. She's smarter and quicker than the pure-breds I grew up with; she had to be to survive in the ghetto.

But the other thing is, she's turned out to be unquestionably loyal and absolutely obedient. And in many ways, she's been my most constant friend in New York.

I NEVER saw the muzzle flash. I can't remember if I even heard the shot. But I knew I was the one that fired because I felt the jolt at my wrists. The familiar recoil sent the gun jerking back, then I saw the guy spasm and fall into the darkness.

The scene froze. Everyone within my field of vision suddenly turned into a statue. And everything had this weird maroon tint to it, like looking through a piece of stained glass. I remember turning towards Tommy, the other cop, up on the row house's stairs. And for a long time he didn't move. His face pale, registering a look of horror and disbelief.

As the haze began to fade, Tommy was the first to move, his face unfreezing and expression shifting just slightly as he turned and began coming down the stairs towards me. But even then, it was in slow motion. Each frame passed agonizingly slow. Every detail sharply focused. The way his hand held the flashlight as it swung. The gun in his other hand at hip level. The equipment on his belt bouncing. It was like a movie without sound.

All around—everyone—cops, people hanging out their windows, myself, we were all moving incredibly slow.

The strange maroon tint narrowed down to a dot. Then everything snapped back. Instantly everyone was moving at normal speed, and slowly I began to hear the sounds.

People were yelling. I was yelling, my voice tight in my throat. I was screaming, "I can't see the gun! I can't see the fucking gun!"

From over my left shoulder I could hear running, other cops coming towards us. They were shouting too, wanting to know what happened. Who'd fired? Who was shot? Trying to sort it out as they ran up on us.

"Put your gun down! Put it down!" Tommy shouted.

I was still "covering" the guy with my gun, holding it out with two hands, ready to shoot again if the shadow at the bottom of the stairs flinched. I screamed back, "I don't see the gun! I can't see the fucking gun!"

"It's all right, man," Tommy said. "It's okay, you shot him."

A sickening panic washed over me. The gun that the guy was pointing at Tommy's face just a couple of seconds ago had vanished. I'd shot an unarmed man.

"I can't see the fucking gun! Get it! I can't see it! Get it!" As the panic rose, I could barely talk. I couldn't catch my breath. The words were coming out strangled as I began to hyperventilate.

Another cop turned me away, pushing my gun down as more cops rushed passed. He was trying to take it from me, but both my hands were tight around the grip, one finger glued to the trigger.

Then someone from below said, "I got it! I got the gun!"

I saw a hand pop up, holding the gun the way cops always hold a recovered weapon. He was holding it up so everyone could see it, like a trophy. Thumb through the trigger guard, two fingers up on the slide, another behind the strap—displaying it like the guy on TV holds the American Express card.

I released the grip on my gun and my partner took it. A moment later they were hustling me into an RMP.

I felt the isolation as soon as the door slammed. I was sitting in the back seat, getting the same view the perps get, only my hands weren't cuffed.

I watched the two cops climb in the front. And it was like a wall went up between us. I could feel them distance themselves from me, not much, but enough. I could almost hear the questions going through their minds. Was it a clean shoot? Did Poss panic? Who the fuck was that guy he shot? If there's a problem—if the shooting was fucked up, nobody wants to know you. But if it's clean, they'd want a little piece of the story to tell.

A second later we were moving, heading towards Jamaica Hospital. Standard procedure; any cop involved in a shooting has to get treated for trauma.

All the way to the hospital I kept saying, "I had to do it. He had a gun. Piece of shit pointed it at Tommy's face. You know, I had to do it."

The cop behind the wheel said, "Relax. Just don't think about it, okay?"

Don't think about it? Relax? Fuck you, I thought. I just fucking shot a guy. Get a grip. But even as I'm thinking this, his partner was on the radio saying, "Five base, you on the air?"

Someone at the precinct responded with, "four," abbreviating the 10-4 to the suffix, just as the cop had foreshortened the 7-5 to 5.

"Make the call," the cop said. "Get a delegate."

As we moved along the empty streets, I remember thinking, "So it's come to this? Why me? Why the fuck me?"

At the hospital they rushed me to the head of the triage line. Blood pressure, medical history, pulse, and temperature. When I unbuttoned my shirt and took my vest off, it was like I was drawing my first breath since firing the shot.

Out in the hallway, the other cops swarmed around me. Protectors, bodyguards. They weren't letting anyone get to me, not before the PBA delegate showed up. And all the time they're reminding me, "Don't say anything. Not a fucking thing."

When the sergeant arrived, I was relieved to see it was Sergeant Glass, a veteran who knew what the deal was and knew to keep procedure simple. I volunteered my revolver without saying anything, and he checked the "state-of-load," acknowledged only one "spent" round, then handed it back. This in itself was a good sign. It signalled to me, and everyone who might have been watching, that it was a good shoot.

If he had kept the gun, it would have meant lost trust, suspicion, and the worst kind of doubt.

Then the intern arrived. Luckily it was a doctor who's known in the precincts. He's an 8-3 cop who's studying medicine, working two jobs. "Do you know your name?" "Do you know what day it is?" "Do you know where you are?" "Do you know what just happened?" "How are you feeling?"

I can tell you this, right from the jump. Maybe they won't admit it, but *all cops* fantasize about shoot-outs. Some of them can't wait to get into a shooting. They have a hard-on for it. Maybe because deep down, that's what they thought the job was all about, cops and robbers. Heroes and villains.

The ultimate scenario is one where you come out the hero; maybe with a nick that draws a little blood, just to show that you're lucky, but still the hero. Unscathed, but salted, cherry-busted.

I had those daydreams. I'll own up to them. Maybe it's all the movies we saw as kids. Maybe a lot of people have those fantasies about coming out the hero. But I never thought it would happen to me, just in my head.

Where the fuck does a kid from Shaker Heights get off shooting anyone?

Shootings are for those other cops. The ones who put in their twenty years and open a bar in Queens. Heroics are for those kids from Long Island, third-generation cops, who'll have a story to tell their friends and families. Maybe it would even be something that brought them a little respect and acceptance.

I didn't know what my friends back home and family would offer me when I told them, but I was pretty sure it wouldn't be a pat on the back and a knowing nod. As it turned out later, a lot of them didn't know how to respond. They didn't even know how to mouth the right words or fake the right attitude. Even for my parents, it was beyond their realm of etiquette.

This is the way it started.

It was one of those sticky August nights where the humidity is pushing up toward 80 percent and everything has a haze over it. Nights like that are markers. You know there's going to be action in the street. People hang out in front of their homes. People start drinking. Everyone's nerves wear a little thin from the heat. Cops, EMS crews, and emergency room staff prepare for these nights on the way to work.

I remember breaking the unwritten, unspoken rule, when I turned to my partner in the rear lot of the precinct and said, "You know, I think something heavy's gonna happen tonight."

It kind of startled him when I said it. Premonitions could turn into omens if you talk about them. It's like asking for something to happen. He kind of gave me a quick look, poked me in the chest, and asked, "You got your vest on?"

On hot nights I've been known to go out on tour without a vest. Maybe it's tempting fate, or maybe I just don't like sweating into it. But on those sticky nights, I'd usually think twice about slipping it on. That night, I didn't. I wasn't thinking about premonitions, but put it on without thinking about it.

We'd just begun the tour when a call came over the radio. A 10-13 (officer needs assistance) citywide, Essex and Atlantic. We tried to get more information, but there wasn't any available. We didn't have a clue what we were dealing with or getting into. It could have been real, bogus, or anything. But then we pulled up to the corner and there was a lone RMP, lights flashing, engine running, doors ajar, and nobody in sight. The scene was eerie, and it gave me a hollow ache right in the pit of my stomach. That's when I knew we'd come into something real.

Then the sergeant and his operator, Tommy, pulled up.

The street was lined with row houses, two and three stories. There was a power station for the elevated subway down at the far corner. It was surrounded by a fifteen-foot-high chain-link fence topped with razor-wire. And there, sitting atop the fence, was a cop. He was straddling the thing, barbed wire right up in his crotch, yelling and directing us by waving his arms— not in pain, but pumped up on adrenaline. He'd tried to follow a perp over the fence and got hung up.

"There's one down there, and two other guys, one went that way and the other over there! They got guns!"

The sergeant and my partner went one way, and me and the sergeant's OP (operator), Tommy, started walking the other way. I'm being cautious, partnered with Tommy, checking porches, between cars, and under cars.

Tommy was walking just a little ahead of me. We both had our guns drawn, and we're working our flashlights into all the dark places. Then I passed this particular house and something hit me. It might have been a noise, something. I turned back and looked into darkness, down a stairway to a basement apartment, and unknowingly, right at the perp.

"Wait a minute," I called to Tommy and he walked back, as I turned my light on the basement apartment's stairway. The light hit right on the top of the guy's head. He was crouched down, concealed by shadows.

I pointed my gun and yelled, "Don't move!"

Tommy jumped the gate, rushed up the front steps, and shined a light on him from above. We saw the gun.

It wasn't hard to spot, it was a black automatic, but the thing that stuck out in my mind was that it had this strip of white tape on it around the barrel.

I took a few steps toward the guy, so that now I'm maybe three feet or so away, and yelled, "Drop it! Drop the fucking gun!"

Then Tommy yelled, "Let me see your hands!"

Soon we were both shouting at the guy to drop the gun, drop the gun, and to see his hands, over and over again. Tommy is above him and I'm two or three feet away, face-to-face and without cover.

It seemed like it went on forever, both of us yelling at the top of our lungs. But the guy didn't move. And the more we yelled, the more he didn't move and the more pissed off I got. Until finally, I'm not even pissed off anymore. I'm still yelling at him, but I feel this kind of despair come down on me. This asshole is just not going to listen. He's not playing by the rules.

We caught him, fair and square. He's supposed to drop the gun, come out with his hands up so we can cuff him, take him back to the precinct, and toss him into the system. That's the way it's supposed to work. But by just crouching there, not moving, he cancelled all the rules.

One thing I know is, I'm not going to jump this motherfucker. There just wasn't enough room. In six years, I've jumped guys with guns, tackled them on the run, and night-sticked them. But with this guy, not a chance. He was down a stairway with a gun out. Even in the shadows I could see his hands wrapped around the stock and his finger on the trigger.

Then the guy did a quick look over his right shoulder, positioning me in his mind, and unbelievably, as we're still yelling at him, with our flashlights on him, he pivoted around and brought the gun up over his left shoulder, so it's pointing right at Tommy's face.

That's when I shot him.

Up to that night I'd handled every call there was: rape, robbery, assault, attempted murder, murder, sodomy, child abuse, child molestation, family disputes, and auto theft. I'd handled maybe three quarters of every felony in the New York Penal Law. With all of those, you just show up and follow Patrol Guide procedures.

Broken window. Door is ajar. Somebody's inside: *burglary*.

Popped door lock. Broken steering column. Broken ignition: *grand theft auto*.

Woman's face is beaten bloody, and his knuckles are bruised: *assault family*.

But when a guy's got a gun and he's pointing it at somebody, you don't think of the charges. You think of what you have to do to stop him. It's on a different level. You're not thinking of paperwork or overtime, or court-tour changes. What you're thinking about is getting the fucking gun away from him. Eliminating the threat.

When a cop shoots someone, procedure puts into motion the department's official machinery. It's like turning on a switch. It begins with phone calls. The DA's office gets a call. The duty captain is notified. FIAU (Field Internal Affairs Unit) is summoned. And the PBA delegate arrives with a lawyer.

By the time we'd arrived back at the precinct from the hospital, an "unusual incident" investigation was in gear. A few minutes later, the PBA delegate showed up, and both he and the nightwatch detectives brought me into the back office to get my story of what happened. They checked the state-of-load of my gun, emptied the cartridges, and made a visual check of each chamber, looking for powder residue that signifies rounds fired.

The full investigation would come later. But little by little the facts started filtering back to me from other cops.

The guy I'd shot and three others had robbed a White Castle at gunpoint. The cops that saw it go down weren't even from our precinct. They were from the 4-7 in The Bronx, "flying" to the Crown Heights riot detail in the 7-1. As they drove by, they spotted guys with guns running out of the White Castle. They didn't know the neighborhood and didn't know for sure what they had, so they put the call out over citywide.

Later, the guy I shot climbed onto the gurney himself. One of the victims from the holdup, after making a positive ID, kicked him. Another spit on him.

A Spanish guy from across the street, hanging out his window, witnessed the whole thing and told the detectives, "I don't know why those two cops kept shouting at the guy? I'd'uve shot the motherfucker right off."

Later, the perp took a turn for the worse. The shot had blown out his shoulder and bounced around inside. It was only a matter of time before he died. A background check showed he was 26 and a recidivist (repeat) felon who'd just finished seven years upstate for armed robbery. He'd been out almost a week.

After a shooting, it's standard procedure for a cop to get a few days off. The department figures it gives you enough time to pull yourself together and to see the department psychiatrist for what's called "early intervention." A couple of days after the shooting, I went and saw the shrink. He asked if little things bothered me more? Was I getting violent around the house? Had I broken anything around the house? Had I taken my gun out at all? Had I dry-fired the gun? Had my eating habits, sleeping habits, *any habits* changed? Did I start drinking or get drunk more than usual?

I gave him all the answers the department needed to assure itself I was sane and stable, which I was. The whole thing, what it meant, didn't really hit me until later. I stopped hanging out with my friends, other cops, assistant DAs, and defense lawyers. I could feel myself withdrawing. None of it seemed connected to the shooting, yet I knew it was.

You just don't shoot someone and walk away. For me it built up slowly, all the anger and all the questions. Strangely, I was even pissed off at the guy I shot. He could have put the gun down, come out quietly, and gone back to prison. It could have gone either way, right up to the time he pointed the gun at another cop's face.

Yeah, right, I'd answer myself back. There you go again, thinking like a white boy from the burbs.

Then there are the personal questions. And for me, there were a lot of them. Another person had ended up dying at my hands. I was born, baptized, and raised a Catholic. What right did I have to take away another man's life? Even as a cop? Even if that person was posing a threat to another person?

The guy was a criminal—a piece of shit. He'd just gotten out of jail for doing the exact same thing. And he was posing a clear threat against another blue uniform, something that stands for law and order. I could be cleared by the department and dead right in the eyes of the law, but there's still that part of me that contends it was wrong.

Four months after the shooting, the letter from the police commissioner's office clearing me arrived. But now, a couple of years later, there's still that conflict. Nothing painful, no sobbing remorse, but irritating and probably there forever.

The dreams about it haven't been nightmares, but more like instant replays. It's not something I think about everyday, but when I do think about it, it's always uncomfortable. And it's always vivid.

What it comes down to are questions left unanswered. It's a test you take and never know if you've passed or failed. It's a feeling of unfinished business. And all the schools you attend, the academies you pass through, the friends you collect, the church sermons you hear, none of them can prepare you for this. And nobody, not your partners, teachers, friends, priests, or your parents can give you the answers after the fact.

Not even my father, who, for everything he's offered, by suggestion or advice, never taught me to pull the trigger.

18

A WHOLE uneventful year passed since the shooting. It slid by in a series of routine busts, radio runs, and everyday bullshit. But within myself I could feel a growing sense of discontentment with the job. When my vacation pick came up, I wanted to put as much distance and as many time zones as I could between myself and the 7-5. Australia.

And when I returned, I came back with a different perspective. For two weeks I lived in a different reality. No violence and almost no crime. All I saw was the rolling surf, beautiful cliffs, and topless beaches. Each day I could feel the 7-5 draining out of me, like a toxin oozing through the sunblock. All the tension, the bullshit, the fear, everything melted away under the Australian sun, washed off by the clear, blue water.

Occasionally, I made calls back home to friends in the States and checked for messages on my answering machine. I'd been involved in a ton of departmental bullshit regarding this one LT, the same one from the firehouse incident. A message left on my answering machine told me that he'd been transferred. And where did they transfer that racist, sexist, psycho-son of a bitch? To a precinct known for its racism, and where the community floods the precinct and One Police Plaza with "civilian complaints." But that didn't surprise me, it was a typical administrative decision.

Sure, the department's being torn in half by racism. People on the street and in the media are calling us racists. You got a genuine racist on your hands, why not send him to a racist precinct? Let him be with his own kind. Nobody was trying to fix the problem, just make it invisible.

My flight back to New York landed on October 10, which was the 7-5's Fifth Annual Medal Day. One of the first calls I made was to another cop in my squad whose father had passed away a few days before. He started telling me about the buzz I missed. How 10,000 cops protested in front of City Hall. And how a couple of papers reported that some of the cops called the mayor (then David Dinkins) a "nigger," "janitor," and "washroom attendant."

Great, so now tension between politicians and department brass spreads to friction between white and black cops.

Then, news got out that this cop, a nine-year veteran and previous partner of mine, was discovered wearing a wire. A fucking wire. First a civilian saw him in the crapper and spotted the wire. That started the rumor, then he got into an RMP accident, and wouldn't let EMS cut his shirt off. That promoted the rumor. So the precinct PBA delegate talked to the CO, who then talked to IAD. Naturally, IAD said it ain't them, that the guy's either acting on his own or for someone else. It took about three seconds for a new rumor to start, that the psycho-racist LT who once favored this cop must've put him up to it. It made sense, a dysfunctional LT attempting to regain some credibility.

The CO relayed this bit of news to the delegate. And the delegate said, we want him the fuck out. Now, what they basically told the guy was, "you're out, pick your precinct."

I never believed the rumors. The guy was my first partner and mentor. Besides, if that was the case—if he was the type to wear a wire—I would have been suspended a long time ago. Not that I engaged in corrupt behavior—but I was a ghetto cop using street methodology to "get the job done."

The rumor eventually turned out to be unsubstantiated. The cop, Eddie, is still at the 7-5, still on midnights.

Even while all of this was going on, I could feel it dwindling down inside myself to the point where I refused to get worked up about any of it. I couldn't take it personally. I wouldn't take it personally.

The first night back, I felt sick. I kept watching the clock. Do I call in sick? Do I tough it out? Finally, at 10:15 I walked out the door like a zombie.

I can't even remember the walk from my apartment to the subway station. There was a time when I wouldn't ride the train to work without my gun. Secured during my vacation, my gun was in my locker. Fuck it, I didn't even remember if I'd left my uniform in my locker or if I was having it cleaned.

I got off the train, walked past the drug locations, and rounded the corner towards the precinct. It was the same, all I'd remembered it to be, it was the same. The same shit-hole.

But something about it seemed unfamiliar. Strange thing to feel about a place I'd worked in more than six years. I felt changed. Damn it, I knew I'd changed. But East New York remained the same. And I'd be fucked if I'd let myself slide back into it.

Down in the locker room I put on my uniform, socks, shoes, gunbelt, not even worrying about squaring myself away. I didn't even check the "state of load" of my revolver, I just holstered it, knowing I'd already missed roll call. Behind the desk I saw an LT that normally worked day tours. He must've been transferred to the late tour while I was in Australia. I'd known him for years as an easy-to-work-with and quiet boss. That eventually changed. The "job" combined with midnights must've turned him shaky. He became wary about OT and obsessed with procedure. He used to be the guy who'd back you up, now it was known you couldn't always count on him.

I walked over, joining the small group that gathers at the back door every night, stalling at the start of the shift. Right away, there's the "vacation interrogation":

"What are the cops there like?"

"Do they do the right thing?"

"What are the chicks like?"

"Did you get laid?"

Always, did you get laid? How much? How many? Who? Did she have big tits?

What they couldn't believe was that the violence that exists in East New York doesn't exist anywhere in Australia. Their cops don't wear bulletproof vests on duty and don't carry their guns off duty. For them to have a gun on duty is a precaution, a weapon of last resort, not a necessity. Those guys can literally close their locker at the end of a day and walk away from the "job." No concern for ever being a victim. And most cops I'd met there had friends who weren't cops. They seemed to have bigger, better lives than New York cops. They had other interests, independent of their work.

For the cops gathered around listening, I might have been talking about some alternate universe.

Handing me a radio, George announced we'd be partnered up as a sector. Right off, we caught a desk assignment: a bias-related thing, someone painting bad words on someone else's door. A shit job and a waste of time. But it figured, I'd been late for roll call, so give Poss the crappy one outta the gate.

We pulled out of the back lot, and my luck continued, it started to rain. A real doom and gloom night, with that chilly October rain coming down. I should have stayed at home.

Just as we were pulling up in front of the house and

about to get out of the car, this other car came racing up, at top speed, and slams on the brakes. Then, this black guy jumped out in a tuxedo. A fucking tuxedo! What's he gonna say? "Pardon me, do you have any Grey Poupon?"

But I only had to look at the guy's face to know it was serious.

"Officer, I'm 'on the job' (police officer) my buddy just had an accident up on the Belt (Belt Parkway)!" he said. "He hit a pole!"

He reached into his pocket and pulled out his shield. He was a Transit cop.

"My buddy's 'on the job' too. He's hurt!"

Now everything's changed. Fuck the house assignment. Cops *always* come first. I got on the radio, reported it as a 10-10 (pickup) job, and told central we'd "check and advise" when we got to the location.

We flew down the eastbound lane of the highway, the cop in the tux following on our bumper. And sure enough, there was the car, on the opposite side in the westbound lane. A VW Jetta with a light pole across its hood and roof.

I jumped out and crossed the highway in nearly shin-deep water, while my partner, George, took the RMP down and around to get to the other side.

When I got to the Jetta, this other black guy in a tux and red bow tie, came up, flashed me a badge, and introduced himself as an instructor in the Transit Academy. And there were more people in the car, two other guys, both wearing tuxes, also probably cops.

As it turned out they were coming back from a Guardian's Association meeting. The Guardians are a fraternal organization of African-American corrections, fire, and police officers.

In the back of my mind, I'm thinking, okay, this is cool. No one's starting any racial tension here. Not a hint of it. So, things can't be that bad.

The driver was pretty young, a PPO. He had a gash on his head, but was more panicked than in pain. He thought he'd lose his job by taking out a light pole. Typical rookie thinking. But he was also hurt pretty bad. His head had broken the rearview mirror and cracked the windshield. Somebody put a handkerchief to his head to stop the bleeding, but he was still going on about losing his job.

My partner arrived then and told us that Transit PD was on its way to assist. Professional courtesy. And that really set the kid off.

"Look, you took out a light pole," I said. "You hydroplaned. Look at that, that's fucking Lake Michigan out there. You hit a fucking pole. You didn't hit another car. Nobody's hurt except you, it's okay. Okay? It's called an acc-i-dent. They happen. Okay?"

"Yeah, don't sweat it," the instructor offered.

"These cops coming, they're Transit," I said. "They're your people. They just want to make sure you're okay. So relax, sit down, shut-up, and keep that rag on your head until they get here."

But he got up again. I sat him down again. And he got up again.

"Look, you're injured," I said. "You're going to have to go to the hospital."

A look of panic spread across his face. "Hospital? I can't go to the hospital! I'll miss training!"

Then the instructor stepped in. I thought he was going to slap the shit out of the kid. But what he did was sit him down, hard, told him to stay put, and do what everyone tells him to do.

Finally, the instructor quieted the kid and about ten other cars showed up. Our LT showed up, Transit showed up, their LT showed up, ESU showed up, and EMS arrived. In the confusion some rubbernecker, mesmerised by the flashing lights and looking for blood, hit another puddle and crashed into the back of another car.

Another sector handled that accident while we stayed with the Transit cops.

As they loaded the cop into the bus, I told him that we'd take care of his car, safeguarding it at the 7-5. We often did this for other cops as a courtesy. I managed to get one of the tow-truck guys to haul it to the precinct's secured lot. He's only authorized to tow off the highway, but since it was an MOS he took it back as a goodwill gesture.

Everything was cool. I really thought I was coming back into some kind of inter-departmental racial situation, but everyone seemed calm. No uncomfortable feelings and the cop's buddies were backing us up on everything we were telling him. If anything, it was just the opposite. At one point, one of the other recruits, also a probationary police officer, kept calling me "sir." Finally I said to this guy, "Look, our badges are the same color. I just have more time on the job than you do, that's all," then stuck out my hand. "My name's Joe."

As we drove away, there were some comments between George and myself, like, "Can you believe how nervous that cop was?"

"Yeah, a real jervous (nervous jerk)."

But whether my partner or I wanted to admit it, we were both PPOs at one time. And did we act like that? Yeah, we probably did.

We finalized the job with central and told "her" we were going "62A" (administrative) over this thing. That would give us enough time to open the lot for the tow-truck guy, do the paperwork, and take a piss back at the station house.

By then I was starting to feel the cold, I was soaked through from the rain and the run across the highway. So before we headed back to the house, I got my partner to pull over so I could get a cup of soup and a tea at Dunkin' Donuts.

Back at the precinct, I secured the cop's car in the lot and headed inside. I sat down to begin the paperwork, thinking that by the time I finished I'd be reasonably dry.

My partner was just walking around, bullshitting with people, killing time.

No sooner did I set my food down than another hysterical black guy comes running into the station house. Now what the fuck is this? Why can't I even eat my soup?

"They're shooting! They're shooting! They just shot my friends!" he said, frantically.

My partner went over and asked, "Who shot your friends?"

"I don't know! Some guy! He was wearing a black hood. Pitkins! Pitkins!" Meaning Pitkins Avenue.

Now, I'm up and moving toward them. "Where on Pitkins?"

"The chicken place, the one over on Pitkins!" he answered, but he can't keep still, pacing and flapping his arms, he can't calm down.

There's more than a couple of chicken places there. Pitkins is a long commercialized street that runs nearly the length of the precinct. "Which one? Which place is it?" George asked, again.

"Queen's! Queen's Chicken!" he answered.

"The one on Miller and Van Siclen?"

"Yeah! Yeah! That's the one!"

It was a guess for me, because there are at least five along that street.

By now, he thinks we don't care, but we're trying to get information from him. And he just wanted to get out the door. He kept pacing, first one way, then the other. It's hard to get a straight answer out of him. Finally he says, "Fuck you! Fucking cops! You ain't gonna help! Shit." And he runs out the door.

Just as the guy's vanishing, the sergeant yelled over from the desk, "Follow that guy. It sounds legit."

My partner and I ran back out to the car, me still carrying my soup. We weren't even out of the lot when the call came over the radio. I got back on my portable, interrupting central, to say that we got the job as a pickup house assignment.

Queen's Fried Chicken was one of those Plexiglass fortified, short-order joints where the walk-in area is for "waiting" only. There was bulletproof glass coming down from the ceiling to the steel counter that extended to the floor. To order food, customers put their money in a reversed L-shaped canal that forms a maze between two panes of the glass. The counter-help slides the food out the same way. The whole place is brightly lit. It's next to a Spanish storefront church, in a line of stores that ended with a meat market, its windows plastered with posters and next to a yellow-fronted bodega on the corner.

When we pulled up in front, I saw three guys lying on the floor. I went over the radio, telling central we needed at least two busses and that there were three males down, possibly shot.

I walked in the door, and there was Mr. Excitable from the precinct. He was still agitated, but glad we took him seriously. And there were three guys sprawled out on the floor. One guy was lying face down on his stomach, shot in the back, and over to his left was another guy, also shot in the back. And over him, lying across his buttocks and thighs, was another male lying face down, not moving.

The guy beneath him was moving a little from the pain, but not much.

When I looked into the kitchen area, cramped with deep-fryers, a Coke showcase of sodas, and some stacked donuts, it looked deserted.

At that point, my partner began to toss the hysterical guy for a gun. Suddenly his mood changed from hysterical to pissed off, "What're you searching me for? They shot at me!"

I started searching one of the guys on the floor, the one in pain, and he started complaining. "What you doing, searching me? I don't have a gun! We're the ones who got shot!"

"I don't know that," I answered. "There's three guys in here, shot, there's gotta be a reason, right?"

"I don't know," the guy said. "I don't know why they shot us."

"Then satisfy my curiosity, huh?" I answered, finishing searching the first guy. Bending over the second guy, I asked, "Yo, you got a piece?"

He said, "No," but made eye contact with his buddy, which told me maybe there was a gun around at some point, but not anymore.

Soon other cars started pulling up with lights and sirens. And outside, a spectator crowd of civilians started to gather. The hysterical guy began telling us this story about how it was one of his buddies' birthday, and they were just out getting something to eat, when this Spanish guy in a "hoodie" came in and started shooting.

I finished searching the last guy, who's dead, and didn't complain. By then, there was blood, a deep maroon color, congealing all over the floor. I couldn't take a step without walking in it.

EMS rushed in, one of the newly arrived cops hustled the hysterical guy out the door as the paramedics went to the closest wall where the two guys were on top of each other.

"Don't bother with the guy on top," I said. "He's dead."

"You sure?" the paramedic asked.

"Well, he ain't moving, and his eyes are open."

As soon as the guy on the bottom heard that, he started screaming and writhing, "Get him off, get him off me!"

Somehow the hysterical guy got back into the store, and heard what I said. Now he starts screaming and flapping his arms in disgust, "Dead! Ah, man, my nigger's dead! He's dead! Ah, man!"

Two cops came back through the door, grabbed him, and pulled him out. "Hold on to him. Don't let him split," I said. "He's a witness."

EMS pronounced (DOA) the guy who wasn't moving. I made a mental note at the time, 1:47 A.M. and took EMS's badge number.

The two techs picked up the dead guy, lifted him off the live one, and dropped him off to the side, right on his face. Then went to work on the guy underneath.

Two more techs came in and started working on the other guy at the far wall.

More people started gathering outside the window. I went over the radio to central, telling "her" we had one confirmed DOA and "Two males serious but not likely," and to notify nightwatch (borough detectives) to respond.

The two live guys were put on gurneys and wheeled out to separate buses. One goes to one hospital, the other to another hospital. I made recorded entries of the hospitals in my memo book: Brookdale and Jamaica.

Now, we've got a witness, a DOA, two injured people, neither of which is likely to die, going to two different hospitals. And someone has to stay at the crime scene to get names, ages, dates of birth, and notify a parent or guardian as to what happened because the males shot were minors. All of them obviously under 21.

The dead kid was dressed preppy. Even more than preppy. I noticed all his clothing was brand new.

I flipped him over and saw that he'd been shot in the chest and that it exited through the back: shot in the stomach: and shot in the abdomen and groin.

More cops started coming in to see the body, commenting on the new clothes. The Timberland boots and Guess jeans, blood-soaked, but still obviously new.

"Nice boots man," one cop said. "Those are *nice* boots."

"Brand new, check'em out," another added.

"Didn't get much use out of 'em," a third piped in.

Another cop, a real joker, put his foot down next to the dead kid's, comparing shoe sizes. "Nope, too small."

Cop humor.

My partner's come back in by then and I said, "You want to go to the hospital or should I?" Somebody's got to go to the hospitals and get the pedigree information. I'm not a sergeant, not officially in command, but, as first officer on the scene, I am.

"I'll go," George said and headed back to the RMP, clearly avoiding the cluster-fuck at hand and dodging the paperwork.

A few seconds later he came back, handed me my soup, and took off again.

People were gawking in through the window. There were at least fifteen people outside looking in and cops edging them back. It was like a big TV screen.

I walked out the door and got some crime scene tape from another RMP's trunk. I tied off one end at the front door, then unrolled it, walking it out to the street, around a parked car, then back to the end of the store, blocking the area off in a chest-high triangle.

Housing and Transit cops started showing up because they heard the call on the radio. Curiosity seekers. And I was just standing there, off to the side of the door, leaning, eating my soup.

Everything at this point was mechanical. A few young girls and some women standing behind the tape staring in were saying things like, "Isn't that a shame," "Isn't it a tragedy?" But it's just noise. Reflex sympathy. They didn't even know this guy. Nobody's crying, nobody's looking away. And all I can think about is, I gotta do this, and I gotta do that, and I got to remember this, and the other thing. Filling in all the blanks for everyone who has to be involved: The patrol supervisor (sergeant), platoon commander (midnight LT), nightwatch,

CSU (Crime Scene Unit), ME (medical examiner), and the duty captain.

Two days ago my world was peaceful. Sunny days, topless beaches, great pubs, and congenial cops with Crocodile Dundee accents buying me drinks. How can these two worlds exist on the same planet?

A few minutes later, the need to notify the DOA's family wasn't necessary. The hysterical guy got to a payphone and called the dead guy's brother. The brother kind of stuck in my mind because he was dressed in a tan hunting jacket and Timberlands. L.L. Bean in the ghetto. He walked under the crime scene tape and into the store. In shock he ID'd his brother, then got on the payphone outside. I could hear him yelling, yelling at his sister to wake-up, wake-up, and wake-up their mother.

Within minutes, the mother and sister showed up. The mother was wearing a blue housecoat, she walked wide around the crime scene tape, looking to pick out anything familiar. Everyone in the crowd watched her, moving silently out of her way. When she saw the new boots and her son, splayed awkwardly on the floor, she went limp.

The sister and brother caught her, holding her up until she managed to get a little strength back. Then she tried to break through the tape and get at her son's body, but the brother pulled her back.

The mother was still trying to get free of the son as the daughter blocked her line of vision and said, "Is that the way you want to remember him? Is it?"

A couple of the cops, sick guys, had this Halloween monkey mask leftover in the trunk of their RMP. They got it out and put it on the kid. Someone started snapping Polaroids, the pictures whirling out, one after another. You see these cops every once in a while, death junkies. Guys with collections of Polaroids of stiffs. It makes you wonder what point they've reached in their thinking.

*   *   *

I showed up at a crime scene once where this guy,
a John Doe Polish immigrant, was beaten to death. Not
shot, stabbed, or strangled, but beaten dead. His skull
was smashed—stomped so hard that his disfigured head
lay flattened across the floor like a rubber mask. Two
cops put a cigarette in his mouth, lit it, and took pictures.

This is real, this is what's going on behind bosses
backs. Not all the time, but sometimes. It's the jokes
that are constant. Jokes and wisecracks; sick humor that
helps you deal with the atrocities.

This is what you don't tell civilians or your family.
How are they going to perceive it? But it makes perfect
sense in the environment. Each time you come face-to-
face with some kid gunned down on the street, there's
this moment of emotional indecision you have to deal
with. How many times can you be saddened and sickened by it? You can sense the sadness, that gnawing acid
sense of tragedy the first time you see a dead teenager.
But what about the twentieth time? You can be shocked,
appalled, saddened, sickened, only so often. What good
is it taking home nightmares of corpses and dead strangers? It's better to reach toward whatever helps you deal
with the situation than take it out of its environment and
into yours.

I used to have a desire to tell non-cops, civilians,
what this is, but even that passed. You can't talk this
feeling into people's minds. You can tell people about
the violence, they may believe you, but they'll never
understand it. Nor can they visualize it. You have to
be saturated with it to the point where it becomes a
part of you. Fed up with it, past disgust. It has to fill
you beyond sadness. Unless you go beyond the pity and
disgust, you can never understand it.

You can walk into a murder scene with every intention of not becoming involved. But it sucks you in,
the job forces you into it. Little by little you learn

this person's life history, pedigree, name, birthday, age, address. Soon you're more than involved in a murder. You see that lifeless face, the last moments frozen in their expression. Their eyes blank. Now picture the person alive.

By getting witnesses and statements you slowly learn who created this havoc. You may not have the perp's name, but you do have a description, and you picture that too. And that is very real. A pool of blood is real. Spent shells on the floor are very real. Witnesses are very real. Their descriptions of what happened are vivid. Everything in that space—the physical space that surrounds the body—is very real. The street corner, the tenement, the store, they all echo with the violence, trauma, and death.

I think, I truly believe, that the person who isn't exposed to this is very, very lucky. They're lucky because they can expend their hopes, energy, and thoughts towards a positive future. They can banish the sanitized version offered to them in the papers and on the news. They can rationalize it to the point where the body, blood, spent shells, and other debris we call evidence are rendered abstract. Or, they can accept it as some distant reality that'll never touch their lives.

Back outside the chicken joint, I started sipping at my now cold soup, thinking about my vacation, and how this shooting was East New York's reminder that the carnage here was constant. But nobody was going to rock my world, not even a little. I bought the soup to eat and enjoy. And nobody would bother me—not other cops; not the gathering crowd behind the yellow plastic tape; and especially not the fucking DOA with those birthday boots. Nothing was going to keep me from my soup. I'll show that fucking stiff in there he didn't interrupt my life.

Now the LT shows up, I told him what I had, boom, boom, boom. This is the information. He's a little "jervous," new on midnights, but he managed to organize the chronology of events.

That's the most important thing, keeping all this information chronological and together—maintaining consistency and accuracy. The procedures get into your head. You just have to keep asking yourself, did I get this information? Did I get that information? And keep checking it off. Check. Double-check. Triple-check.

"My partner's at Brookdale Hospital," I told the LT. "Suggestion Lieu, you might want to send someone to Jamaica Hospital. The body that went there was the more serious of the two." Always a "suggestion," because a cop never tells a boss what and what not to do.

"Good idea," the LT said and it got done.

Then the duty captain showed up, and I repeated all the facts and details. Names, ages, the time EMS pronounced the DOA, the fact that we have family of the deceased at the scene. We have complaint reports for all the victims. I have aided cards for all injured, and appropriate departmental notifications have been made. I don't have complete information on the guy who went to Brookdale, nor information on the guy who went to Jamaica, but that's being taken care of; I'll have it later.

I'm still sipping at my soup. Even this duty captain, a "white shirt," isn't going to stop me.

I asked EMS to give me a white sheet to cover the DOA, but as soon as the sheet hit the floor, it soaked through with blood.

Back outside I called the precinct from the payphone. I have to get four aided numbers, because I have three injured complainants and one DOA. Three 61 (complaint report) numbers, actually 4, but the fourth guy, Mr. Hysterical, he's alive and I can get to him later. I need all these numbers because when nightwatch shows up, they want the name of the first cop and his partner on the scene. What sector they were designated, RMP number, how the job came over, who EMS pronounced dead, EMS's number, what the 61 numbers are, what the aided numbers are, notifications and to whom they were made, names of witnesses if any, and a brief synopsis of the events and a description of the perp. And if the perp was known to any of the victims. Are they willing to talk? And where are they?

Nightwatch eventually showed up and I got some polyester detective throwing me rapid fire questions. "Whatdowehavehere?"

I started to tell the story.

"Wait. Wait," he said, pulling out a pad and pen. "Who's that guy on the floor?"

"That's the victim. He's DOA."

"How many shot?"

"We got one DOA, two, no, three," I said. He's starting to get me confused.

"What? Waitaminute, start over."

"Two others shot, serious but not likely, at two separate hospitals. And another complainant not shot."

"Waitaminute," he said. "HowmanyDOAs?"

"One DOA, two shot, serious but not likely. They're at two different hospitals."

"Whatdowehavehere?"

And I started to explain it again. Finally, he gets the information down. "Who's the DOA?"

I gave him the name, age, date of birth, where he lived, the time of pronounced death, and the fact that his mother, brother, and sister were right outside.

"Do you have 61s for me?"

"No, not yet because we don't have the names of the other two victims. But they're coming soon." It's like he expects a miracle to fall from the ceiling.

"What happened?"

"Well, according to the witness . . ."

"Whoa, what witness?"

"I said, there were four guys total, two injured, one dead, and a witness."

"Where's the witness?"

"Outside in an RMP."

"Well don't let him get away."

No shit, Einstein, I thought to myself, but said, "No sir, someone's watching him."

I wanted to throttle this fucking cheese-eating, brown-pants, blue-short-sleeve-dress-shirt-wearing asshole.

What happened was this. It was the DOA's birthday. He'd just turned 20. Those new clothes he was wearing were his birthday presents. He got to wear them for a total of maybe three or four hours.

After his party, the dead kid and his friends went out to get something to eat. They went down the street to get take-out food. They began to order, when this male Hispanic, wearing a baseball cap and black hoodie pulled over the rim, walks in and opens fire. He hit three, the fourth fell to the ground, pretending to be shot, and plays dead.

Now, this is the strange thing, I got seven shells recovered, and several deformed rounds in the Plexiglas. Two of which went through the supposedly bulletproof divider, taking out a glazed donut, the other laying in the Coke cooler.

Also, I have a whole bunch of questions going through my mind. Who was this guy who shot them? Why did he shoot them? This 20-year-old who just spent his birthday with his family, why did he die? Why did the others just get injured? And why did this hysterical cocksucker who ran into the precinct, leaving his shot buddies behind, have the common sense and "cool" to pretend like he's hit and play dead on the floor? Unless, somewhere in the back of his mind, he's a dirty son of a bitch and ready to drop at any given moment, if it even looks like someone's going to shoot him. He's the one who was probably the mark, the other three just not-so-innocent bystanders. And what about that suspicious look one of the shot victims gave this guy when I tossed them for a gun. Someone had a gun.

The detectives hung around, detecting. The crime scene guys came, took their pictures, and gave me various pieces of evidence to voucher.

After the crime scene techs left, it was time to recover personal property off the DOA. On went the rubber gloves, the dirty job was mine. Another reason George probably took the hospital assignment.

The family was gone at this point, they were told to go home and directed to call a funeral home to make arrangements through the morgue at KCH (Kings County Hospital).

I picked him up and rolled him over onto his back. First I removed his watch. A black Swatch type of watch. Black with white numerals. I took it off and put it in the bag. He had twenty bucks in his pocket, blood soaked. Keys, to an apartment probably, also bloodied. No wallet, nothing else.

By the time I'd finished, the gloves were blood-covered. Peeling them off without getting any on you is a trick. Take them off, drop them to the floor.

That's what gets me about crime scenes. The crime happens, all the equipment rushes in, and when they leave, they leave all this debris, neck collars, torn clothes that have been cut away, bloodied gauze, and used packages behind. Medical things. Medical debris.

And inevitably, someone asks, "What about all this stuff?"

"Hey, what do I look like, a janitor?"

"Who's gonna clean it up?"

"Not me."

What we found out later was that the kid that was killed was clean. Absolutely clean. He'd just passed his NYPD exam. He wanted to be a cop. His friends were clean too, even the one who pretended to be hit. In a precinct where they solve better than eighty percent of the homicides, so far this one is unsolved. But it could have been anything, one of the kids could have been a dealer who wasn't busted for his first time; one of them might have just looked like somebody, or maybe even gave a bad look. In East New York, it's possible, even probable, to die because you looked at somebody the wrong way.

Who cares? The murders will be solved or they won't. Somebody will go to jail for it or they won't. There will be a trail or there won't. Justice will be done or it won't. Whatever happens, that kid will still be dead.

By tomorrow afternoon, the crime scene tape will be down, and all the evidence of the murders cleaned up from the front of the store. With any luck, they'll be open for business by lunch. When George got back from the hospital, we started putting our information together. I'm writing information on the back of my memo book, reminders. But right now, all that needs to be done is to have the body removed.

If the body is in plain view, on public display, EMS will come and collect it; if it's in a private place, like an apartment, you have to wait for the morgue techs from the ME's office to come in a beat-up, blue van, and remove it.

This one, EMS took out of professional courtesy. Two techs brought out the "scooper," a metal stretcher, that opens at the center to grab the body, then closes, securing the body. They took the body away, driving off in the misty rain.

Years later, that night would probably become a pivotal date that marks the passage of time for the family, like a birthday or wedding anniversary. The next time the family sees the kid would be in his best suit at the funeral service. That is how they would like to remember him.

But for all the strangers who looked in through the window and all the people who would hear about it the next day, his death was incidental. He will not be remembered.

For the EMS techs, nightwatch, and all the cops, he was another body for the system—another tragedy for the system to process. A few facts of his life, and detailed technical facts of his death, will be recorded in case files and reports. Within a day or two he will be reduced to paperwork.

THE DAY after the shooting at Queen's Fried Chicken, I went to KCH morgue with my partner, George, to ID the body. A couple of day-tour cops gave us a ride over.

To reach the morgue, you have to pull into the hospital's entrance, and make a sharp right turn down a ramp into a small parking lot. The guard on duty waved us through and we parked the RMP next to the ME's blue van.

The entrance to the morgue has battered swinging doors, like an emergency room, that open into a nondescript tiled hallway. The whole place has a dreary city building quality to it: functional, battered from constant overuse and abuse. It doesn't look much like a hospital—no gleaming white tiles, bright fluorescent lighting, or sterile quality to it. It looks like the basement of a YMCA. Except for a few gurneys lining the hall, used as makeshift tables to hold medical supplies, you could be anywhere—a prison, a precinct, or the Department of Motor Vehicles.

As you enter the morgue itself, you anticipate the smell. You wait for it, expecting it, but the smell doesn't come until the end of the hall when the morgue attendant opens the door to the refrigerated storerooms.

Then you start to smell it, not overpowering, but subtle, everywhere—a strong medicinal hospital smell mixed with decay. Sharp and heavy at the same time. It's formaldehyde, disinfectant, and chemicals. It's decomposing bodies, body fluid, stomach compost, and internal organs. Once you've smelled it, you never forget it. The scent lingers on your clothes, getting into the fabric, and your nose, so that hours later you can still catch a whiff of it.

Set into both walls are the stainless steel doors of individual refrigeration units, like on TV. Each about two feet by two feet, the units are secured by lever-locks that catch best when the doors are slammed shut. At the far end is the *Science Room*, called that because it was once used to store organs and "spare parts" awaiting analysis. It's a refrigerated fifteen-by-twenty-foot room. If you donated your body to science, the room was a layover stop before medical school and dissection in gross anatomy class. Now it's used primarily for storage, extra space for extra bodies. It was empty that day. At the opposite end is the *Green Room*, which got its name because it's filled with gurneys holding the decaying bodies of unidentified John and Jane Does in zippered plastic bags.

Anonymous and unclaimed, this is where indigents are held before being transferred to the docks. They're then taken by ferry to Hart's Island, New York City's Potter's Field. There, they're buried in numbered pinewood caskets in mass graves, dug by prisoners.

What you see a lot of lately, and it's sad, are babies and children. AIDS babies, premature babies, children who've died from neglect and abuse, falls from a window and stray gunfire.

Most cops head for the Science and Green Rooms, wanting to see what new horror the city has produced. Testing themselves to see if anything can shock them. The morgue attendants are used to it. Oddly, they accept this human fascination with death. They even encourage it. If a big case comes in—something that made the papers or television news—they'll proudly point out the body. Yeah, that stiff's a celebrity, our celebrity.

The bodies lay naked on gurneys, sometimes in body bags, sometimes covered by sheets, but most often they just lie there exposed. Time has turned the bodies green, blue, maroon, yellow or purple. Ethnically, most are Black people. Unidentified.

After awhile, you become proficient at spotting causes of death. Just by looking at the body, the circumstances come to you. Drug shoot-outs or planned hits. AIDS cases. Knife wounds. Fires. Car crashes. Blunt instrument traumas, and suicides. And all of them, with that crude morgue stitching and stapling that closes the chest cavities.

In one corner was a woman, the skin and flesh peeled from her forehead and pulled down over her jaw, exposing bone and teeth. On another gurney was a head, just a head.

"What're you trying to do, put a name to a face?" I asked. Cop humor, but everyone's heard it before.

A couple of assistants were walking around, and when they saw us, in uniform, their eyes flashed to the collar brass. For morgue guys, the numerals of a precinct on your collar stick out. More than a hundred murders a year from the 7-5 pass through their facility. Murder in the 7-5 never surprises them. A lot of 7-5 cops get to know the morgue attendants, by face, if not on a first-name basis.

I can remember the first body I saw in the 7-5, murdered on the street with two bullets to the head. It looked unreal. My mind rebelled from it, making it look like an actor in a movie, but knowing this was it— the worst thing that can happen to a person. I'd seen bodies before, but this one was out on the street, in the territory of the living. He was sprawled face down in the street, fully clothed, and all alone. He could have been a discarded vacuum cleaner or mattress from the way he appeared carelessly tossed there. Yet, there he was, a human being lying on the pavement.

I looked at him for a long time, knowing that the vacant lot, the chain-link fence, the buildings, were probably the last things he saw. He was walking down the street before two bullets to the back of the head turned him off as neatly as flipping a switch.

After my tenth DOA, the emotions dissolved. I stopped thinking about the horror of it and started thinking about the OT. This was normal. Some cops in the 7-5 will race twenty, twenty-five blocks, eighty miles an hour, lights and sirens going, crossing entire sectors, just to reach a murder victim first. That body is money. Worth at least five to six hours of OT. Cops with a reputation for "body jumping," will key their mics, cutting off other responding units, snatching the job from central. Guys'll jump on the radio before the dispatcher can finish describing the job. All it takes is a "10-10 shots fired, male down . . ." or a "10-54, male shot . . ." and they're on the radio, mics keyed, like some caffinated "Jeopardy" Grand Champion.

If there's a tie between two units at the crime scene, then a little negotiating may be called for. If the sergeant or LT responding isn't a hardnose, he may gratuitously hold two units at the scene, awarding both OT. But the idea is to get there first, set up the crime scene tape, claim the body, and win the OT.

We headed upstairs, signed in, and told the clerk what we were there for.

"You in a hurry?" the guy asked.

That's the question posed by city employees everywhere. The morgue guys know, cops on OT are never in a hurry. If you're on the clock, then you'll be there for awhile. Paperwork can take as long as you want it to. And after awhile, that's what bodies mean, paperwork and OT.

I shrugged, then George shrugged, meaning no reason to really hang around more than necessary.

The guy told us that the body had already been ID'd by the family and the autopsy performed. Then he brought out a Polaroid, a picture of the kid's face with a blue plastic wrapping around it. The expression on his face was one of surprise. Not horror or shock, just surprise. A homicide face.

This kid's mouth was open, lips back, and two gold-capped front teeth exposed. His eyes were wide open; like he was about to bite into an apple.

If you're a member of the family, a morgue attendant will bring out the body for you by itself. Treating the family with courtesy and the body with respect, like a viewing, but they'll do it in a neutral zone. Not in the Green Room, where the family might see other horrors brought in and tossed on gurneys. And not in the cutting room, with its steel tables and surgical instruments. In any of those places, the family would likely hear the echo of a radio tuned into a rock or rap channel, or attendants cracking jokes. Instead, they'll do it in a hallway or empty room somewhere and speak in low tones.

In the office I ID'd the photo and signed a witness form. On it is written the deceased's name, time of death, and location. At the bottom are our names, rank, shield, command, time we made the ID, and the name and signature of the doctor who performed the autopsy.

Since the shooting the night before, he'd entered the system. The body, autopsy findings, and bullets they dug out of him—everything—was now part of a chain of evidence. He'd become a statistic. Another single-digit number that moved the 75th Precinct up a notch, edging us into another record year of homicides in the city.

The guys who gave us a ride over didn't want to wait out in the RMP. They wandered inside the Homicide Investigations Room adjacent to the morgue office. They were checking out the Green Book, a big thick volume, like a captain's log on a ship. The Green Book is filled with photos of the victims downstairs in the Green Room, past and present. Opposite each picture is a full-page description of how the body was found, cause of death, and any newspaper articles relating to the case. Overwhelmingly most of the people in the book are black.

They were looking at the book to see if anything could shock them. But after awhile, nothing shocks you.

There's a burn victim.

Yeah, but what about that burn victim without a head?

What about that head without a body?

What about that body without a head, shot twelve times, and hog-tied?

When you've seen it enough times, nothing raises that human pity and sense of disgust, or whatever else it is you're looking for in yourself. What act of cruelty, mutilation or violent death can surprise or shock when you already know what people are capable of doing?

One of the attendants asked, "You guys in a rush?"

Everyone shrugged.

"They're doing an autopsy downstairs."

It's kind of a macho thing, nobody wanted to say "no." It's a morbid curiosity. We've all seen autopsies, but maybe this one is the one that gets the other guy to lose his lunch or reveal something we haven't seen. The one that goes beyond whatever line we've crossed a long time ago.

We followed the guy downstairs to the cutting room. Inside were four slightly tilted steel tables with raised edges running along their sides. A couple of bodies were layed out, waiting.

As we walked from the first table to the last, the attendant offered a running commentary. Pointing he said, "He was caught in cross fire. Six or seven bullet holes."

Thumbing at the next guy, the attendant said one word, "AIDS."

We all walked wide on that one, keeping away from the withered body of a man who couldn't have been more than 30.

Approaching the next table his tone turned sarcastic. "Next one. Shoot out. He lost." No shit.

At the last table, where the pathologist was, lay a female. Light-skinned Hispanic, maybe 25. A suicide. She shot herself in the chest, blew her own heart out. Big dark hole in her chest, a stippling of gunpowder shadowed around it.

She must have been a good-looking woman when she was alive. A thin scar from a C-section ran across her lower stomach. She *was* someone's mother.

Leaning into the semicircle we'd formed, one of the cops whispered, "Would you fuck her?"

A moment's hesitation, then one of the other guys said, "Yeah, I'd fuck her."

"You'd fuck her?" feigned shock.

"Well, not *now*! I mean, when she was alive."

There was something pathetic, absolutely sad in this. Here's this woman, her life on a path so bad and hopeless that putting a gun to her chest and pulling the trigger seemed the best of all possible choices. And here's four cops, looking at her, laid out, lifeless, wisecracking.

The pathologist, an Indian guy, ignored us and made the first cuts that form a "Y," from each shoulder, connecting at the sternum, then follows down to the thatch of pubic hair. The scalpel was so sharp it separated the skin with just a light touch. Both breasts came to rest at opposite sides of the torso.

We watched with grim fascination as he cut the chestplate away with an electric saw, then lifted it out, placing the square mass of bone and cartilage at her feet. With the internal organs exposed, he could now follow the bullet's path. Here and there he made notes on a pad.

Her chest completely opened, he reached in with this huge stainless ladle and started spooning thick, congealed blood from the cavity. Internal bleeding. The blood was so dark, it was nearly black. Cupful after cupful, he dipped in, then emptied it between her legs, letting it run down into the drain.

When he was done with her, there were three more bodies to do. Like a factory. Cut, cut, cut. Weigh this, weigh that. He worked mechanically, knowing what to look for. And he was good at it; he probably did eight to ten bodies that day.

We signed out of the morgue, and on the way back to the precinct we all stopped for Chinese food.

When I was working on my senior project in college, I went to see an autopsy at the suggestion of Frank and Shine. Again, I think they were trying to shock the college kid.

Instead, I found it fascinating. Here was this body, a stranger's body, and the pathologist and his assistant were taking it apart trying to find out exactly what made him die. All those organs, the things we never think about, until one of them fails. All those organs that work together, *that have to work together*, in order for a person to live. And how we take it all for granted.

The other thing that stuck out in my mind was the pathologist was eating—fucking eating—while he performed the autopsy. There he was, with a gloved and bloody hand, reaching for a Sprite, a straw protruding at just the right angle from the can. Between cuts he munched on a Grandma's soft oatmeal raisin cookie that was wrapped in a napkin.

At the time I was really shocked by his blasé attitude in the face of death. *Now* if I saw that, I wouldn't flinch. The guy in front of you would be dead, whether you're hungry, thirsty, or not. Life goes on.

My grandmother died during my junior year in college. I got the phone call that temporarily interrupts your life, but doesn't stop it. She was old, her health deteriorating, and ready for it. The last time I saw her, there was very little left of the spirited grandmother I had known all my life, the one relatives called "Red," because of her vibrant auburn hair in her youth. The one who baked homemade Toll House cookies for me from scratch. It was her time. And her death was natural.

My grandmother's life took a natural course, following a predictable chain of events. She was born, she crawled, then learned how to walk. She grew up in healthy, wealthy, and comfortable family surroundings. Well-educated and meticulously refined, she finished school and married my grandfather in Roman Catholic tradition. She had three children—Peter, Paul, and Mari. Then her children had children, and she saw her lineage continued.

When she died, it was a personal, family tragedy, but not surprising. The loss wasn't wrenching, we expected it to be natural. Age had become a burden for her. The loss was our loss because we would miss her. But she'd spent her life well, squeezing everything she could from it.

In East New York, death can, and frequently does, come unnaturally. It can come when you're 4, 12, or 16, when life's hardly begun. When a kid's shot on some street corner, it's violent. Bullets enter his body, smashing bones to splinters and ripping up internal organs. It's unnatural, the last minutes filled with pain and fear.

Everyone in the ghetto knows it can come at any time—cop and civilian. If you're 15 years old and killed in drug-related cross fire, it isn't a surprise. Depending on who you are, it's seen as a tragedy, bad luck, deserved, or just another statistic. But not an overwhelming surprise. Not in East New York.

That's exactly the place we've gotten to in East New York. In Brooklyn. In America. We've reached a point where the violent death of a teenager no longer shocks us. Where there is no more emotional trauma left in it. We've created an environment of complacency, where tragedy is the everyday currency of the media—where television, newspapers, and magazines are our national Green Book.

We watch in morbid fascination to see if anything is able to touch our emotions . . . to move us to action.

EPILOGUE

. . . **AND IN** the end, there is nothing I can tell you.

I have worked in the midst of such despair that it would have been impossible for me to imagine such a place before I arrived and saw it for myself. The enormity of it is staggering. The memories of it, soul-killing.

To think that the devastation didn't happen over night, but slowly, over years, is to ask: Why didn't somebody stop it? To believe that it was allowed to happen is to admit to the unconscionable about ourselves as a society.

I have seen dead infants, killed by a parent's hand, abandoned and left to die or tossed like trash down a garbage chute to fall eight floors into refuse.

I have seen children hit by gunfire. The image I carry around is of a child, maybe 2 years old, zipped into footsie-pajamas. The child is laying in a bed, in some housing project bedroom, soaked in a dark pool of blood, killed by a stray bullet, that pierced the window as the family slept.

I have seen dead teenagers, killed by other teenagers. The bodies on gurneys. The shooters locked in nine-by-twelve steel cages or out on the street.

I have seen women brutalized, beaten bloody.

I have seen men brutalized, stomped to death.

For years I have seen people who have reduced themselves to animals by their need for drugs. Night after night, women from the nearby shelter, toothless emaciated crackheads, climb into the sanitation trucks that line up along Stanley Avenue. In the trucks, they perform oral sex on sanitation workers. The price is three, four, and five dollars. They move from cab to cab, getting just enough to keep them high for the night.

I have delivered a baby in a tenement hallway, easing it out into stench and filth.

And I have lied to the dying as they bled on pavements, telling them it was going to be "okay." I have beaten the shit out of those who were surely guilty, never once feeling regret.

I have witnessed these horrors, acquired the images, accepted the reality, and made myself an active player in these events. Just as cops across the country have witnessed and played a part in them. Like other cops, I know there is no time limit and no goal beyond the immediate. There is no end to any of it.

You cannot say there are 1,000,000 illegal handguns in New York, and when you take one away there are 999,999. There is no finite number of crack vials or guns. They seem to materialize out of thin air, multiplying themselves like a virus. Like a plague.

There are still a few cops who want to fight the good fight in places like East New York. They are the true believers. But they are helpless against the machinery of the system and the turmoil in the street. And they are not the majority of cops. Whatever the media, the politicians, and the police brass say, believe this: they are not the majority of cops. If they cannot be excused as rookies who don't know any better, they are labeled as loners and outcasts by their peers.

Most feel they're lucky to "put in their twenty" and buy a bar with their pension money or work as a square badge (security guard). If they're lucky they'll have a life after "the job" in which to tell stories about being "on the job."

For the unlucky who stay too long, even their cop cynicism burns itself out to passivity, so that by the time they're pensioned off, they're emotionless and bloodless ghosts.

The city wants more cops. There were 28,000 when I joined the force. Now there are 36,000. And they're talking about 40,000 by the year 1996.

Will 40,000 be enough? I doubt it.

What about 50,000?

Will 75,000 be enough?

How many prosecutors? How many judges? How many prisons?

How large does the system have to be before it solves our problems?

In the end you spend so much time devoted to something that you think will progress, convinced that you can make it better, until finally, you're overcome by it. I thought I could do it, chip away at a piece of it. But now I know that I can't do it. I no longer want to do it. I don't want to even attempt to do it.

I have learned that there are no more trials for justice here. Prosecutors and defense attorneys make bargains in desperate expediency. There is no time in the courts, no room in the jails, no longer the desire to seek order by law. Whatever ideal of justice we once held has been rendered a luxury.

Justice has been reduced, finally, to the level of the street. Justice has become a ghetto cop who's lost faith in the system, jacking a guy for resisting or gun possession. He does this because throwing a beating to the scumbag at least guarantees a personal verdict, personal justice. But it also validates the payback of a drive-by shooting and all the other ghetto carnage. These are what pass for law and order here. It is through these things that our human desire for punishment, retribution, and justice must be satisfied.

I'm only human—cops are only human. But this is much bigger than one 30-year-old cop in the 7-5. I could die out there and nobody, not one person, would be saved. Mine would be a useless death, added to all the other useless deaths.

I look at people my parents' age and see them remembering what was, not comprehending what is. They have no point of reference for any of it. The impact of what has been created in places like East New York does not register. How could it?

Six and a half years in East New York taught me that the force and momentum of it are overwhelming. Ultimately, I learned that the brass and the politicians don't send you out there to make a difference. You're sent out there to keep the ghetto in the ghetto. You're sent out there to mediate, to be the barrier between an inaccessible system and the public. But most of all, to generate numbers. Because the machine, the department, wants "numbers": arrest numbers, homicide solvency numbers, and summons numbers. The numbers show effort and action. They are the proof against the evidence of daily reality that the machine works. They generate revenue and reassure the public. And a reassured public re-elects its officials.

Somewhere, I am sure of it, there are those in office who read the murder stats like stock market quotations. They display the income from summonses and the rise in homicide solvency on computer-generated charts. They study their bar graphs and pie charts and think they are winning. Then they go home to places where they are safe, and their children are safe. They retreat to homes and communities beyond the reach of a hopelessness they don't want to know.

They send you out there and say, "Okay, play cops and robbers." And you do, moving through emotional changes in the process that take you from eager rookie to burned-out street cop.

At first I was gung ho. I wanted to learn the job, learn the street, and do the best I could. And for awhile I did. It was exciting and fulfilling. There was the illusion that

I was making a difference. I was fighting crime, kicking crime's ragged ass. And after I saw the hopeless reality of it, I decided to turn that experience and expertise into an OT franchise. I became hooked on the adrenalin and the money. For years I was one of the highest earners in my squad. I became greedy and learned how to work the system: *Collars for dollars*. In my best year, I made $60,000, more than a third of it in OT. I averaged three or more collars a week and cashed in on more than my share of DOAs. It's like that in most every precinct, ten percent of the cops making ninety percent of the OT.

For all the years I worked, I remained unaware of the price I was paying. The environment was toxic and there is no professional training that can prepare or protect you against it. *No one is immune*. You can't rationalize away what you have seen. And you can never forget it.

Today, there is an innocence in me that is lost, gone forever. That saddens me. There is no place inside of me that this job has not touched. My entire world has been colored by it. I've thrown up a wall of callousness, suspicion, and mistrust around myself. Whatever I have left of what I was before, I'm now looking to protect.

When and if I ever get married, I want to be happy and festive. If my wife or child dies, I want to cry at that funeral. I desire to have some of these emotions left for the important things in my life. It scares me to think, now that my parents are getting older, what is going to happen when one of them passes away? Am I going to cry for them? I don't cry for people in the ghetto. My parents are closer to me, of course, but if they do die in my lifetime, I don't want it to be just another death. I want it to be a *loss*. I want to feel it, question it, and know my grief is genuine, to know it's authentic.

Strange thing to realize that a piece of yourself can arrive DOA in your life, without warning.

* * *

The saga of East New York, with its decaying landscape of urban wreckage, murders, robberies, rapes, guns, drugs, and other violations of the Penal Code, continues. At this moment crimes are happening in the 7-5 that are not being witnessed by cops. Burglaries, rapes, robberies, shootings, drug transactions are taking place all over the precinct . . . all over New York City. RMPs are moving through the streets, going to crime scenes, and passing future crime scenes. Crowds are gathering to view the body, the accident, the fight, the latest tragedy. Cops are interviewing victims and beating perps. All of it was there before I arrived, and it was there while I wore the uniform.

It is happening now.

When the orders came through assigning me to the 7-5, I was relieved. I'd made it! My *permanent* command.

I was living in Port Washington at the time, a beautiful suburb of Nassau County along Long Island's North Shore. I called up the precinct the day before I was scheduled to report for duty to get directions. And that was a little weird because the PAA (police administrative assistant) couldn't relay specific directions. I was transferred from one extension to the next, then transferred again, until finally a cop who lived near Port Washington got on the line and gave me directions.

I remember easing off the Belt Parkway and onto Pennsylvania Avenue. It didn't look so bad. But as I drove and drove, the scenery began to slowly change. Block by block, the buildings, the stores, the apartments, everything began to look more and more run-down. Instinctively, I knew that I was passing the ragged edge of the ghetto.

The whole time I was driving, I noticed that these people were looking at me. I mean really *looking* at me. At stop lights, at stop signs, in traffic. It was a nice summer day, I had the sunroof opened and the radio tuned to a rock channel.

There I was, a white boy driving through the ghetto listening to The Doors in his Audi Quattro 4000.

Finally, after about twenty minutes, I gave up looking for Sutter Avenue and pulled over next to this parked police van. I turned down the music and popped my head out through the sunroof.

The cop on the driver's side of the van looked at me. I remember wearing Raybans and a new blue Brooks Brothers button-down. His stare went from me, to the car, then back to me.

"Excuse me, I'm looking for the 75th Precinct," I said.

The cop turned a little courteous, the way they do when they're talking to civilians who really don't have a major problem. "Do you know where you are?" he asked.

"I'm lost," I said, smiling. "I'm a cop. I'm gonna be working in the 7-5."

The cop's expression went a little blank as his eyes again went from the car, to me, then back to the car, then back to me. He turned and said something to his partner, who nodded.

I was just sitting there, with my head popped out of the sunroof, feeling like a rookie asshole.

"Look, you better follow us, okay?" he finally said.

"Sure." Now, this was hospitality.

I waited until he started the van, then followed him back into traffic. But about three blocks up, he ran a light and we got separated. I thought I saw him make a right turn . . . or did I? Second-guessing myself, I made a left, went four blocks, decided he'd made a right after all, then began doubling back, only to get more lost in a maze of one-way streets.

Suddenly, I'm in a place that doesn't even look like New York. Thousands of people are out on the street, kids, old people, young people. Cars are up on jacks, others "stripped," supported by cinder blocks. Every half block a little kid ran out into the street, or I'd hit a pothole. And I'm passing what I'm sure is drug location after drug location.

Finally, I saw all these police cars parked next to a building. But the cars looked a little funny. Not the same white and blue as in Manhattan, but orange and navy. I stopped and went inside. I found out this was "Housing" PSA #2 (police service area). They got me going in the right direction. I U-turned and headed down Sutter Avenue. Again, the landscape seemed to worsen with each block.

When I finally reached the 7-5 station house, I couldn't believe it. There was a small crowd gathered outside, people just hanging out, and dogs, ghetto strays, aimlessly wandering around. Cars were parked up on the sidewalk, and sirens were blaring every two seconds.

I parked in the rear lot and walked in through the back door. I just stood there for a long time, nobody paying any attention to me. It looked like a trauma ward after a plane crash. Uniforms, detectives, and civilians rushing around. Cops pushing handcuffed perps through the roll-call room. Two or three more perps were chained to the wall. And everyone's shouting, cursing, and talking at once—like a scene out of "Hill Street Blues."

I just stood there, holding my uniform on a hanger, taking it all in. These weren't cops like I'd worked with in Manhattan, these guys were different. They moved with a sureness that a lot of cops in the city only feigned. And, they had this air of menace and fatigue. I suppose war vets call it a fifty-mission stare. But it was more than that. These guys had a fifty-mission attitude.

Ghetto cops.

Compelling True Crime Thrillers
From Avon Books

THE BLUEGRASS CONSPIRACY
by Sally Denton
71441-8/ $5.50 US/ $6.50 Can

FREED TO KILL
by Gera-Lind Kolarik with Wayne Klatt
71546-5/ $5.50 US/ $6.50 Can

TIN FOR SALE
by John Manca and Vincent Cosgrove
71034-X/ $4.99 US/ $5.99 Can

"I AM CAIN"
by Gera-Lind Kolarik and Wayne Klatt
76624-8/ $4.99 US/ $5.99 Can

GOOMBATA:
THE IMPROBABLE RISE AND FALL OF
JOHN GOTTI AND HIS GANG
by John Cummings and Ernest Volkman
71487-6/ $5.99 US/ $6.99 Can